"[This is] a book about much more than social medi... you feel you have lost your way in a noisy world, this book will help you. If you feel overcome by your attachment to the numb of the scroll, in these pages you will find hope.

God has a plan to meet with you—a fresh revelation He wants to speak into your soul. Of that, I am sure. While this fast might at first feel like a tremendous sacrifice on your part, it's really a huge gift from Him."

From the foreword by Lisa Whittle, bestselling
author, speaker, podcast host, and ministry coach

"It's almost impossible to be still and hear the voice of God with the relentless hum of technology in the background. I love that this book invites us—in fact, gives us permission—to tune out social media and turn toward the Savior instead for forty days. As you set aside this sacred time, get ready to hear from God and replenish your soul. You won't lose much by ignoring social media posts, but you have much to gain when you seek God!"

Arlene Pellicane, speaker, podcaster, and author
of *Screen Kids and Calm, Cool, and Connected*

"Our thoughts determine our beliefs, our beliefs determine our attitudes, and our attitudes determine our behaviors, so what we spend time thinking about impacts both how we feel and ultimately how we behave. A decade ago precious little time was spent on the internet; whereas today, social media profiles are growing exponentially and online surfing comprises more of our day than spending time gathered around the table for family meals. *The 40-Day Social Media Fast* is a challenge to all of us to turn from what our behavior proves is our first love (all things online) to the One who desires to be our first and only love. Wendy Speake helps us to see that in and of itself, social media (or food, or music, etc.) is not inherently bad, but when we turn to it to cope rather than to the God with all wisdom, we trade that which will last for eternity for the momentary gratification of a "like," a ping, a calorie, or a tune. If you've found yourself growing disenchanted with life, I'd recommend you read *The 40-Day Social Media Fast*, and intentionally and purposefully reengage with the One who died to have a relationship with you."

Dr. Michelle Bengtson, board certified clinical
neuropsychologist, national and international
media resource for mental health and wellness,
and award-winning author of *Hope Prevails*,
the *Hope Prevails Bible Study*, and *Breaking Anxiety's Grip*

"It's hard for me to overstate how badly we need this book and how badly our families need this book. I long to go to Jesus more than my phone. I long for my children, one day, to go to Jesus more than their phones. We need help to keep technology in its rightful place, and this book is precisely the kind of help we need. Wendy is gracious and humble, and she speaks with authority and kindness. I've always wanted to take a social media break but couldn't get up enough nerve to do it alone. Thanks to this book, I'm not alone. Thank you, Wendy, for blazing the trail as we set the phones down and look to the One who gives true life."

Jessica Smartt, author of *Memory-Making Mom*

"If you are done being distracted and sucked dry by a scrolling device that doesn't really satisfy, you need *The 40-Day Social Media Fast*. Wendy helps us discover the joy of real-life devotion to the Lord, our family, our coworkers, and the amazing world around us that we so often miss because we're a generation that lives with eyes glued to our phones instead of eyes up to God and the people He's gifted us. There's a better way. Get ready for change!"

Becky Keife, author of *No Better Mom for the Job*

"Over ten years ago I never would have left home without my keys and purse. Today I make sure that more than anything, I never leave home without my phone. It's the first thing I check when I wake up, the last thing I look at before I go to sleep, and the one thing I glance at more times throughout the day than anything else. Although my smartphone has smart features that help me throughout my day, I find that my brain feels more crowded now than ever before. My neck aches from looking down, my eyes feel the strain of staring at a screen for much of the day, my shoulders are cinched up from the stress of it all, and my spirit . . . my spirit feels empty and drained. After reading *The 40-Day Social Media Fast*, I knew that although I can't completely remove technology and social media from life, I need to take a step away from it all and adjust how I get through each day. This is a wonderful book that reads easily but is abundant in rich content!"

Jenn McClure, @thebooknest.boxbus

40-Day Social Media Fast Testimonials

"One thing the fast taught me was that I was reaching for my phone instead of reaching out to God. It was so freeing to live my life for the past forty days, instead of reading about everyone else's lives!"

Angela D.

"These forty days have been fabulous. I realize that I need connection . . . with people somewhat, but especially with my Creator. It's been the most joyful, laughter-filled, life-giving time I think I've ever experienced! I will continue to fast from social media and only be present on my business page!"

Allison C.

"The enemy takes advantage of not only the distraction social media offers but also the comparison it encourages. Thank you for sharing your heart and giving us tools to help us grow closer to the Lord!"

Christina S.

"During the 40-Day Social Media Fast, my big focus was on increasing my prayer life. Specifically, I felt the Lord calling me to stop and actually pray in the moment with someone when they ask. I don't think it's a coincidence that during the fast one of my pastors (who knew nothing of my new goal) asked me to join the prayer team for alter calls! God is obviously at work, growing me and stretching me, which is both scary and exciting."

Susan C.

"I enjoyed this social media fast so much! The first four or five days I couldn't believe how many times I clicked on the Facebook button out of habit. As the days went on, I created *a new habit*. Bible study. Since then, I've been in the Word daily. I'm praying more and feeling much more refreshed."

Kelli K.

"Jesus first!"

Shawnda R.

THE 40-DAY

Social Media

Fast

Exchange Your Online Distractions for Real-Life Devotion

WENDY SPEAKE

BakerBooks
a division of Baker Publishing Group
Grand Rapids, Michigan

Published by Baker Books
a division of Baker Publishing Group
PO Box 6287, Grand Rapids, MI 49516-6287
www.bakerbooks.com

Printed in the United States of America

Library of Congress Cataloging-in-Publication Data
Names: Speake, Wendy, 1974- author.
Title: The 40-day social media fast : exchange your online distractions for real-life
      devotion / Wendy Speake.
Other titles: Forty-day social media fast
Description: Grand Rapids, Michigan : Baker Books, a division of Baker Publishing
      Group, 2020.
Identifiers: LCCN 2020036158 | ISBN 9780801094583 (paperback) | ISBN
      9781540901194 (casebound)
Subjects: LCSH: Internet addiction—Religious aspects—Christianity. | Social media
      addiction. | Social media. | Spiritual life—Christianity. | Christian life.
Classification: LCC BV4596.I57 S74 2020 | DDC 261.5/2—dc23
LC record available at https://lccn.loc.gov/2020036158

The author is represented by the William K. Jensen Literary Agency.

20 21 22 23 24 25 26   8 7 6 5 4 3 2

This book is dedicated to those of us who want to want God most but grab our phones more.

Pursue the things over which Christ presides. Don't shuffle along, eyes to the ground, absorbed with the things right in front of you. Look up, and be alert to what is going on around Christ—that's where the action is. See things from his *perspective.*

Colossians 3:1–2 MSG

Contents

Contents

Foreword

What God wants from us, He also wants for us.

For six months leading up to December 1, 2019, I knew God wanted me to take a break from social media. I felt that internal nudge, the silent but persistent Holy Spirit one.

After some reluctance I agreed. There was more to it than just feeling like I *couldn't* fast from social media. I didn't *want* to. With tendencies toward overworking, my night brain is occupied like a pesky hamster that runs my mind wheel to death, and scrolling seems to tame it. Let's be clear: I enjoy the numb of the scroll.

But all my resistance to fasting was pointless, because if there's one thing I've learned in my forty-eight years, it is that Jesus sticks with His plan. God had a plan for me to quiet my phone and listen to Him. In the middle of the first night after the detox started, He spoke an important revelation to my heart.

I wish I had said yes to God sooner. In a world full of loud and persistent human voices, it has become more dire than ever to hear from Him.

It brings me joy to be the one to welcome you to my friend Wendy's book—a book about much more than social media fasting. If you feel you have lost your way in a noisy world, this book will help you. If you feel overcome by your attachment to the numb of the scroll, in these pages you will find hope.

God has a plan to meet with you—a fresh revelation He wants to speak into your soul. Of that, I am sure. While this fast might at first feel like a tremendous sacrifice on your part, it's really a huge gift from Him.

Remember, what God wants from us, He also wants for us.

I'm so excited for you to begin.

Lisa Whittle, bestselling author, speaker,
podcast host, and ministry coach

Before You Fast

We all seem to be looking down these days. I wonder if that's why many of us feel down too. We perpetually bow our heads, but not in prayer. While we might believe prayer works, we don't have the time to get on our knees because we're on our phones. Checking in online, responding to a text, watching a YouTube video—then looking up just in time to snap a picture of the sunset. As we post it to social media, we realize our neck aches and that we forgot to switch out the laundry.

We need a break. A holy hiatus. A social media sabbatical.

My name is Wendy, and I'm exhausted. Perhaps it has something to do with late nights spent streaming movies, or maybe it's because I don't have any quiet moments without a screen stimulating me. I'm all tweeted out. I need to unplug for a season so that I can plug in to the One who seasons me. I want to be salty again. I want to be light-bright too, with energy to serve and smile, but I'm as drained as the battery on my phone—and I know I'm not alone.

Here's the backstory about how I came to fast from social media in a backward sort of way: Six years ago, I invited my online "friends" to join me for a forty-day sugar fast. I was astounded by the number of people who signed up for our online community. Progressively, year after year, more

We need a break.

A holy hiatus.

A social media sabbatical.

men and women joined us for the annual event. We confessed, collectively, that we were turning to something other than God's strength to get us through our days. So we fasted from sugar in order to feast on Christ and His sweet Word. Each time we journeyed through those forty days together, He grew in us a holy hunger for Him. He was increasing in our lives, and we were decreasing. Many of us dropped pounds, but more than anything else we dropped our idols. Some of us even dropped our phones.

While sugar is the emphasis during that forty-day fast, fasting from sugar opens the door to our sweet Savior. We invite Him into the innermost chambers of our lives. Once inside, He looks around and says, *Thanks for the sugar, but I want it all. I want your whole life.* At that point we ask ourselves what other distractions are distracting us and what other strongholds are holding us back from experiencing His strong hold. In chorus, the majority of my fasting friends respond, "It's my phone!"

Smartphones distract us from focusing on what matters most: God. And the real-life friends He's surrounded us with come in a distant third. Throughout the pages of this book and the days of our fast, we'll return to Matthew 22:36–39, where an expert in the Levitical law asked Jesus, "Teacher, which is the greatest commandment in the Law?" This man was really asking Him, "What matters most?"

"Jesus replied, 'Love the Lord your God with all your heart and with all your soul and with all your mind.' This is the first and greatest commandment. And the second is like it: 'Love your neighbor as yourself.'"

Nothing in my life has made loving God with all my heart, soul, and mind more difficult than my constant connection to my devices. The same is true when it comes to loving my real-life neighbors. Devices are divisive.

Ten years ago, I would wake up, stretch, and pick up my Bible from my bedside table. Well rested, I spent time with God at the start of each new day before seeing to the needs of my three young children. It was my morning routine. Today, however, the first thing I reach for is my phone. Though I promise myself, "I'm going to open my Bible app," and often I do, my "quiet time" gets interrupted by noisy notifications from people I'm connected with online. Connecting online has made connecting with God nearly impossible.

Before I know it, I'm checking email, and then I hop over to find out who liked my Instagram post from the previous night. As my shower heats up, I interact with the virtual friend who left me a message as I slept. At the start of each new day I communicate with those I "like" more than I do the One whom I love most, which begs the question, Do I truly love Him most?

I believe in my heart that I do. I love God more than I love all the people in the world (and all the people on the World Wide Web), but the habitual way I turn to the world testifies to my priorities. That's why *The 40-Day Social Media Fast* is my own personal journey back to what matters most—*Who* matters most.

C. S. Lewis wrote, "Human history [is] . . . the long terrible story of man trying to find something other than God which will make him happy."[1] Today in this digital age, with our smartphones, tablets, watches, and laptops beeping at us constantly, we are desperately looking for happiness. In Jeremiah 2:13, the Lord calls out: "My people have committed two sins: They have forsaken me, the spring of living water, and have dug their own cisterns, broken cisterns that cannot hold water."

If you find yourself constantly thirsty for more, never quite satisfied no matter how often you go back to draw from the well of social media or online streaming and shopping, then you've likely been drinking from a well that was never meant to satisfy you. Like it or not, we all tend to forsake the spring of living water and dig our own cisterns. They're broken and, as a result, so are we. Still, we keep at it. And the more broken we become, the more fervent our search for happiness.

Each ping, buzz, and notification triggers a dopamine release in our brains, synthetically creating a short sensation of happiness. We've become chemically and emotionally addicted to these short-lived highs. That's why I've decided to put my foot down by putting my phone down, so that I might pick up the joy-inducing presence of God instead.

I'd venture to say that you originally picked up your phone as a resource to enhance your life, not to consume it. However, the brilliant people who designed Facebook, Instagram, and countless other social media sites are masterminds at cultivating addiction. Our online world has not evolved accidentally; it's been engineered intentionally. I feel it personally as I pick up my phone one hundred-plus times a day. I see it in my children as they play online games and send snarky memes to friends. I witness it as my husband sets his phone faceup on the table as we gather for dinner as a family.

We're all struggling to live in the moment as a result. We struggle to interact with those we love, because we're chasing after those we "like." We forget to actually smell the roses we're busy taking pictures of. What's more, the pixelated glow of our screens does not cause us to shine in the world as Christ called us to shine. I've already warned that we can lose our saltiness, and now I'm saying we can lose our shininess too. But I refuse!

Those are a couple of the reasons I decided to take my first social media sabbatical. I wanted more than a fleeting feeling of happiness; I wanted lasting joy. So I deleted the distractions and devoted myself to finding it. The first place I looked was up, and it turns out that looking up was the answer. Now I'm lifting my eyes again and inviting you to look up with me.

WHAT THIS BOOK IS AND IS NOT

The 40-Day Social Media Fast is a collection of forty daily readings intended to lead you back into the presence of the One who matters most. This fast isn't merely a digital detox, though you'll experience that too. This is a spiritual fast with a deeply spiritual purpose. We are taking a break from everyone else in order to make room for Christ and those He has placed in our lives. John Piper wrote, "True freedom from the bondage of technology comes not mainly from throwing away the smartphone, but from filling the void with the glories of Jesus that you are trying to fill with the pleasures of the device."[2]

This book is not a treatise on the evils of social media. I'm not here to convince you that you're struggling in this digital age. Instead, this book and these forty days are an invitation and opportunity to make room for the glories of Jesus.

A recent study determined that every second there are eleven more people logging on to social media for the first time. By 2021 it's estimated that more than three billion people will be connecting online. That's 40 percent of the world's population. And I'm not talking about just "checking in." The average time individuals spend social networking continues to climb as well: 109 minutes a day in 2015, 126 minutes a day in 2016, 135 minutes a day in 2017, 144 minutes a day in 2018, and 153 minutes a day in 2019. At this rate, by the time this book is released people will be spending, on average, nearly three hours of their daily lives online.[3] Of course, we don't need statistics to know it's true. That's why we're setting our devices down for forty days.

A social media fast is not about keeping technology in its rightful place. Oh, no! **This is about keeping God in His rightful place: at the center of our attention and affection.**

HOW TO BEGIN

Throughout Scripture, we see that the Lord clearly speaks to those who seek Him. He spoke to His people through angels and dreams, through the law and the prophets, and at last through Jesus Himself. Because God became a person, He knows how to speak personally, and that means He will personalize this fast just for you if you allow Him to. He won't give you a to-do list (or a to-don't list) and send you on your way to muscle through alone. Take the specifics of this fast to Him, and then allow Him to guide you through it with the help of His Holy Spirit. Perhaps the Lord will speak to you about one or more of these online temptations:

Facebook: Are you tempted to abide on Facebook instead of abiding with the only One who said, "Abide in Me"? If that's the case, then make this a Facebook fast. Lay down Facebook and lift up your face. Put down Facebook so that you might spend some undistracted time face-to-face with Him. Your face in His book: that's the Facebook you need right now.

Instagram: If those beautiful little squares hold you captive, give them up and spend time with the One who gave up His life for you. If you find your worth in the perfectly curated images you share on Instagram, spend these forty days considering how you were made worthy in Christ.

Twitter: Have you bought into the lie that "You are what you tweet"?[4] Spend forty days discovering who God says you are. Your identity is not found in how witty or pithy your 280 characters can be. You are a child of God, made in His likeness. Shut down Twitter and open up your Bible. Spend your time digging into the Word and discover who you are there, based on God's opinion.

Netflix: It's not social media, but this site can suck your night hours dry. If you forego your nightly rest in lieu of a story line not your own, dive into God's story and the narrative He's writing in your life. Shut down the fictional characters you spend hours with each night and invest that time in real-life people, right where you live.

Online games: If you spend more time playing "Words with Friends" than you spend exchanging words with your friends and family, give up those games for forty days. When you stop focusing on leveling up, there's a chance you'll look up.

LinkedIn: Do you find yourself checking to see who in your industry is searching for you online? Quit LinkedIn for forty days and quit obsessing about your next job. It's your job now to cease from striving and ladder climbing.

Online work: Speaking of work, people often tell me they can't fast from social media because much of their work or ministry is done online. Take the specifics of this fast to the Lord. He knows your job. Perhaps He'll speak to you about putting parameters around your work hours, such as budgeting a half hour to posting and communicating with clients online at the start of each workday, followed by another short slot at day's end. Then stay offline the rest of the day.

That said, God may call you to do something even riskier. One of my friends owns a small business online, and during our fast she felt led to shut down her business completely. I understand that isn't an option for most people. I share her story only to demonstrate that when we incline our ears and our hearts to hear, our Savior speaks to each of us in a personalized way.

There are thousands of other apps, social media sites, and online time sucks—virtual rabbit holes we tend to fall down each day. Snapchat and Pinterest, TikTok and online dating sites, podcasts and TED Talks, Instagram stories and Facebook Live videos, texting and emailing without end. While you might want to send me a DM to say, "We can't stop communicating altogether," my response would be, "We already have."

All this "communicating" has stopped us from communicating with the One (and the ones) we value most. I know this feels countercultural, and indeed it is. But Jesus said if we're going to follow Him, we must deny ourselves (Matt. 16:24). For the next forty days, stop following everyone else online so that you may follow Him with all your heart.

Exchange your online distractions for real-life devotion.

Guidelines

As you prayerfully take this fast to the Lord, list specifically what you're laying down and consider how you hope to fill those empty spaces with the glories of Jesus. Throughout your fasting days, the Lord may ask you to surrender something more. Do what He asks: obey. He has not called you to make a social media sacrifice but to be a living sacrifice (Rom. 12:1), so stay alert to the convictions that will surely come. Next, choose when you will fast, and invite your family and close friends to join you. Here are a few ideas for when to fast:

January: January is a beautiful time to step back from the hectic pace after the jam-packed holidays. The fact that it's the start of a new year makes me think of God's call to bring our firstfruits to Him. The first forty days is a little more than 10 percent of the year. In a way, we are tithing our words, our attention, and our focus. Jesus gets more than His share up front, first and foremost.

Lent: I personally choose to step back from social media each Lenten season. It's the time of year when Christians traditionally fast from food in order to feast on Christ's presence. Since I have found that I mindlessly nibble on a virtual feast more than any literal food, I annually set down my devices during these holy days. This fast has become so meaningful to me, I eagerly anticipate it the way some people look forward to a literal vacation. The Lenten season has become my annual virtual vacation.

Summer: Summer is another sensational time to fast from screens. Moms especially use their screens to sneak away and take a rest from all the people in their homes, all day every day. What would happen to your summer and your memory-making if you spent it with your hands free? Would you be less occupied with others and more present with your people? Less sharing your fun and more having fun?

Tuck these forty days anywhere into your year. Perhaps you'll enjoy the break so much, you'll log off again before the year is through. No matter when you take your social media sabbatical, I pray that you find great joy and freedom when you look up!

Additional Resources

Download a digital detox checklist, screensavers and decorative prints, scripture memory cards, and other free resources to help you prepare for your screen sabbatical at 40daysocialmediafast.com.

DAY 1

Is Social Media Bad?

"Why do you call me good?" Jesus asked him. "Only God is truly good."

Luke 18:19 NLT

Whenever I suggest to people that they spend a prolonged season fasting from social media or sugar or shopping or dating—anything that distracts them from their intimate relationship with the Lord—I get the question, "But is it bad? Is social media bad? Is sugar bad? Are dating and shopping and eating and drinking all bad?" The answer, of course, is both simple and complicated. No, these things aren't bad . . . and yet perhaps, for you, they aren't good. Instead of asking, "Is this good for me?" start by considering Jesus's words: "Only God is truly good" (Luke 18:19 NLT).

Of course, God, in His overflowing goodness, has given us many good things to enjoy. As a matter of fact, in the creation story, He looked down upon all He had made and "saw that it was good" (Gen. 1:10, 12, 18, 21, 25). So, what did Jesus mean when He said that only God is good? I believe He meant that every good thing is only good in light of the good purpose God created it for. Plants and animals are good as plants and animals, phones are good as phones, and relationships with loved ones are good in their proper place as well, but none of these things were ever intended to replace God. The sun was never meant to be the Son. Gifts were never supposed to take the place of the Giver. No created thing in this world was meant to replace the One who created this world. That would be bad.

God looked down on all He had made and enjoyed His creation. Of course, He wants us to enjoy it too. So, no. Food and drink and dating and reading and shopping are not bad in and of themselves. Nor is social media, unless the created gets in the way of the Creator. If social media has gotten between you and the Lord, then social media is not good for you.

Over the course of these forty days, you may discover, as many people have as they fasted and prayed, that social media, online games, and streaming movies are not good for you. Perhaps you will learn to set boundaries around your time online—what you share, when you share, why you share it, and how often you check back to see who liked it. Fasting from social media for a season may help you understand your relationship with both God and your phone.

First Corinthians 10:23 tells us that all things are allowed, but that doesn't mean they are necessarily good for us. I love how *The Message* version sums it up: "Looking at it one way, you could say, 'Anything goes. Because of God's immense generosity and grace, we don't have to dissect and scrutinize every action to see if it will pass muster.'" The point is not to pass muster as we pass through life but to live life in Christ to the fullest. Does social media help you to do that?

C. S. Lewis once wrote, "There is no neutral ground in the universe: every square inch, every split second, is claimed by God and counterclaimed by Satan."[1] Our good God wants to use social media for our good and His glory, but Satan is hell-bent on owning that territory and using it for our distracted demise. This is true in everything. God wants us focused; Satan loves us frazzled. God wants us devoted; Satan loves it when we're distracted. God wants us content; Satan loves us discontent—dissatisfied, depressed, and dejected. God wants us to know His incomparable love, while the devil wants us comparing our lives with others as we search for a different sort of love—a love that looks more like "likes."

The greatest good you'll ever experience is the all-surpassing love of God found in Christ Jesus! Is social media bad? No, but our human tendencies are. **If you habitually look for love and companionship online, when the love of God is found in the companionship of Christ, then social media isn't good for you.** Perhaps you need a short forty-day break to connect with God. Disconnecting from that which is less good frees you up to connect with the One who is most good. With His help, when this fast is over you might be able to set boundaries around your online relationships that allow you to enjoy those good gifts in light of the good Gift-Giver. But if you can't, then don't reengage online. All things may be allowed, but if they don't allow you to stay focused on the satisfying goodness of God, then they aren't good for you.

Social media isn't the enemy, the devil is. Social media is simply another spiritual battlefield. The devil wants it for himself, but the Lord wants everything that touches our lives to be a holy touch from Him. He has good purposes for every good thing He's made. The devil knows it; that's why he is always on the hunt—looking for opportunities to take the ground beneath our feet. He is referred to as "the prince of this world" (John 14:30), and as our enemy he "prowls around" the whole world (and the World Wide Web) "like a roaring lion looking

A life spent in fellowship with God isn't just a good life, it's the best life.

for someone to devour" and a clever way to devour them (1 Pet. 5:8). He uses everything this world affords him.

These words by A. W. Tozer challenge me profoundly: "Whatever keeps me from my Bible is my enemy, however harmless it may appear."[2] In *The Screwtape Letters*, C. S. Lewis tells the story of a senior demon named Screwtape who is teaching his nephew, Wormwood, a young demon-in-training, how to entice a man away from Jesus. One of his main tactics is to distract the Christian from Christ. I would love to read a modern-day retelling of this classic.

Is that thing you hold in your hand separating you from the One who holds you in His?

In light of today's technology, how would Screwtape advise Wormwood to lure his man away from God?

Has social media distracted you from the devoted life? Has it prevented you from experiencing an abiding fellowship with God? **A life spent in fellowship with God isn't just a good life, it's the best life—and that best life segues into a forever life of eternal fellowship.** How wonderful! Fast from that which feels good temporarily in order to experience the only One who is good eternally, who holds your best life in the palm of His gracious hand. Is that thing you hold in your hand separating you from the One who holds you in His?

Is social media bad? No, maybe not, but for the next forty days, let's set it down under the lamplight of Jesus's words: "Only God is truly good."

Dear Lord, You are good and good for me, and You desire to grow me up to be good, just like You. I need more time with You, Lord. I don't want anything to get in the way of that sanctifying relationship. Thank You for these forty days. I am choosing You, the good Gift-Giver, over any good gift. In the good name of Jesus, Amen.

DAY 2

Follow Me

"Come, follow me," Jesus said, "and I will send you out
to fish for people."

Mark 1:17

I t's possible that the people you follow online have come between you and the One who said, "Follow Me." This isn't a hypothetical statement. I know it to be true for myself. Unless I intentionally follow Jesus, I unintentionally drift along with the masses in this world's current. But Jesus didn't simply swim upstream; He walked on water. He rose above the cultural currents of the time and invited His closest companions to join Him above the waves. He said, "Come, follow me" (Mark 1:17).

He invited His disciples to follow Him at the beginning of their friendship, and after that He kept inviting them, over and over again. Consider Peter, who received his very first "follow me" in Matthew 4:19, then heard it again after Jesus asked three times, "Do you love me?" (John 21:17, 19). **Jesus does not offer a one-time invitation but a constant wooing.**

Matthew 14:22–33 tells the story of Jesus walking out upon the windswept Sea of Galilee. As He approached the boat that held His friends, in the hazy moments just before dawn, the disciples saw Him coming and were terrified. "It's a ghost!" they cried.

Jesus, who is always calling us up to greater faith, responded, "Take courage. It is I. Don't be afraid."

Peter, impetuous and bold, shouted out to Him, "If it's you, tell me to come to you on the water."

"Come," Jesus invited—just as He had at the start of their friendship, on the shore of that same lake. In response to this predawn invitation, Peter stepped out of the boat and walked above the current's pull. Unfortunately, the wind and the waves rallied to catch his attention, and Peter, distracted, took his eyes off of Jesus. Afraid and sinking, he cried out, "Lord, save me!"

It's possible that the people you follow online have come between you and the One who said, "Follow Me."

Immediately Jesus reached out His hand and caught him. "You of little faith . . . why did you doubt?" He asked (Matt. 14:31).

Here at the start of your 40-Day Social Media Fast, it is my hope that you hear our Savior's familiar call: "Come, follow Me." Whether you are standing on the shore, having never before responded to His invitation, or are sitting in your little boat eager to walk with Him above the pull of the culture's current, the invitation is yours. Join Him.

It won't be easy. The temptation to take your eyes off of Christ and His buoying Word will be constant. Loneliness may even threaten to capsize you, but what a joy it will be to step out of your boat and follow Him in this countercultural, faith-building, water-walking way! Over the course of these days, you'll need to keep your eyes continually on Him or be swept away. That's why His invitation is ongoing, rather than once-and-done:

"Come, follow Me."
"Follow Me."
"Come ..."

How gracious of the Lord to keep inviting us still!

Perhaps, in recent years, as the world's waves have grown larger and louder, you can't hear Him as you once could. If that's where you find yourself today, I understand. However, I have learned from experience that it's not because the Lord has grown quiet; the world has simply gotten so loud it drowns Him out.

Though I turn to the Lord in the quiet morning moments as I read a passage of Scripture and a daily devotional, the majority of my day is spent in the clamoring conversation online. I'd like to say it isn't true, but the proof is on my screen. My iPhone tracks my time online, testifying to my priorities. Seventeen minutes on the YouVersion Bible app at the start of the day, followed by 163 minutes on social media, news threads, and texting. No doubt, my eyes are on the wind and the waves, and my ears are attentive to those I follow online.

While Jesus clearly said, "Come, follow Me," I wear myself out following everyone else. Perhaps you're tired too, and ready for a rest. Jesus extended this invitation in Matthew 11:28: "Come to me, all you who are weary and burdened, and I will give you rest." While I memorized this verse years ago, recently I've felt the Lord speak this invitation to me in light of all the other things I run to, turn to, or "come to" each day: *Come to Me.*

As I turn on my computer: *Come to Me, I want to connect with you.*

As I make a phone call to talk through my stress with a friend: *Call on Me!*

As I scroll through Facebook: *Don't follow them, follow Me.*

As I open up Instagram: *Come to Me, open up to Me.*

As I binge watch another late-night TV show: *Come. To. Me.*

As I start a text, complaining to a friend about my day: *Delete that; don't complain to her, come to Me.*

As I link over to Amazon Prime for a little retail therapy: *Come to Me, I'm a Wonderful Counselor.*

As I run in to Starbucks for something sweet: *My words are sweet as honey. Come to me.*

As I turn to comfort food: *Come to Me, I'm the Great Comforter.*

Come to Me.

There are so many things I mindlessly turn to each day—so many things I eat, read, watch, buy, and consume. But God's invitation to His disciples was, and remains, "Come to Me. On the beach, on the waves, on the hillside, in your home—wherever you are, I Am. Come to Me."

Are you weary? If you're worn out and wiped out, exhausted from running to all the false gods this world has to offer, run to the One who invited you to bring your weariness to Him in the first place. He can carry your burdens. The One who shouldered the cross can shoulder what concerns you today. It's what He does, what He came for. Amazon Prime can't do it. Facebook can't do it. Netflix can't do it. And all the people you're following online can't do it either. It's not their job to lighten your load or brighten your countenance. It's God's job. *Don't follow them, follow Me. Come to Me.*

The One who shouldered the cross can shoulder what concerns you today.

He is able to carry your hurting relationships. He can handle your fears and your failures. He can shoulder your loneliness too. He alone is able to relieve you of your sin-struggles and your shame. He can carry the weight all the way up Calvary's hill and lay it down at the foot of the cross on your behalf. In exchange for those heavy burdens, He offers His light yoke. That's what He gives us when we give it all to Him.

Do you like the idea of "coming to Jesus" but you're not sure what that even looks like? Then follow me in the pages of this book as I follow Jesus. Take a moment to accept Christ's gracious offer and let Him lead the way these forty days!

Dear Lord, Your Word isn't a far-off record of an old and distant God. You are speaking today to my listening heart, "Come to Me." You're inviting me now. Holy Spirit, give me the courage to stop opening my phone and instead open my ears to Your quiet voice. I've been stubborn, but I'm so grateful for Your oft-repeated invitation, "Follow Me." Nothing else has ever been able to get the job done. Only You have that power to meet my needs as I follow You. And so I'm praying in Your name as I say yes to following You today. Amen.

DAY 3

Escapism

"Haven't you read," he replied, "that at the beginning the Creator 'made them male and female,' and said, 'For this reason a man will leave his father and mother and be united to his wife, and the two will become one flesh'? So they are no longer two, but one flesh. Therefore what God has joined together, let no one separate."

Matthew 19:4–6

Grandma passed away on my twenty-fifth birthday. Of all the women in my life, she best modeled for me steadfast devotion to one's husband. Grandpa wasn't perfect, and neither was she, but she remained a devoted wife through wartime, followed by a lifelong marriage. Grandma did, however, have one passion that lured her away from her family. She loved to read. When she

---

Note: While this book isn't written specifically for married couples and parents, the focus of this chapter is on those relationships. If you are not married or don't have children, I hope you'll read it and apply its lessons anyway. We all have stressors we'd like to escape from time to time, and the online world is an easy escape route for us all when we grow weary of our real-life challenges.

needed a break from Grandpa's big personality (or her rambunctious grandkids), she'd disappear into the bathroom with a library book.

Over the years, Grandma checked out so many books from her local library that she came up with a system to prevent herself from accidentally checking out the same books multiple times. On page thirty-six of every book she read, she'd underline the page number in pencil.

While she always had books scattered throughout her house, I don't remember ever seeing my grandmother reading one. She never had a paperback covering her face when I was in the room. Not when we painted with watercolors at the kitchen table, not while I swam in the pool, and not as we watched a show together. It was always her face that I saw.

Just as Grandma made sure there was never a book in her face when she was with me, I try to keep my face out of Facebook when I'm with my family. Over the years it's gotten harder and harder. I am very much like my grandma, with quiet sensibilities, and my husband is like my grandpa, with endless energy and charisma. What's more, we have three equally strong children in our home, with constant questions and loud voices. As an introverted, highly sensitive person, I get overwhelmed regularly, and social media is a tempting way for me to escape the stress. Unfortunately, when I pull away for a few quiet moments online, I rarely come back rested and ready to reengage.

When I turn to my phone to cope with stress, I don't return to my family more able to handle the stress.

When I turn to my phone to cope with stress, I don't return to my family more able to handle the stress. When I sneak away to social media, I don't return to my husband and children more socially available. When I put my face in Facebook, rather than the Good Book, I don't find the help I need when it's time to face my family again.

Back when my oldest was four years old and my youngest was a newborn, I started turning to Facebook on my desktop computer during their afternoon naps. When the children woke up, I'd shut it down and leave it in the office. Because I'd not used the time to prep dinner or put away laundry, I always felt a bit guilty, but even so I was able to leave my distractions behind in the other room and dive into family life again.

Things changed when my phone outsmarted me. Once Facebook had a permanent place in my pocket, it became a permanent portal—able to transport me away from my family. Even if we were physically in the same room, I wasn't necessarily there with them. Facebook was no longer simply a naptime vacation but an all-day form of escapism.

The effects on our marriages are doubly compounded because our spouses have their own virtual rabbit holes offering them an easy escape route as well: text threads with friends keep them laughing, and the news can get more of their face time than we do.

When Jesus spoke of marriage, however, He told His followers not to let anything separate them from their spouse. Matthew 19:5 tells us that a husband will leave his family and be united or *hold fast* to his wife. I've always loved the King James Version word choice: *cleave*. God created us to leave and then cleave. Unfortunately, in this present culture, we leave one another and cleave to the wrong things.

The Hebrew word for cleaving is *kollaó*, which comes from the root word *kolla*, meaning glue.[1] This isn't your run-of-the-mill white school glue. This is spiritual superglue that binds us together, making us one. To separate from each other requires a ripping so intense that shards of the one remain embedded in the other. That's why divorce and estranged relationships with kids are so painful. Today, however, many of us leave without leaving—we leave our families and cleave to our phones. Escaping our loved ones was never God's plan for us.

Leaving our phones and computers in another room is a good first step, but most of us don't set such a precautionary boundary.

When we don't make the choice to leave our temptation behind, we're making the choice to allow the temptation to remain. It's hard to *hold fast* to someone when you're holding your phone. Hopefully this fast will help you to hold fast to your loved ones again.

When one of my friends returned from our community-wide social media fast, she exclaimed, "These past forty days, my children saw my face more. That alone made it so worth it!" I have heard similar statements from many parents after fasting. Not only did their kids enjoy them more, they enjoyed their kids more. I'd venture to say that many of those kids even became more enjoyable. When our children have our intention, they don't need to get our attention. Andy Crouch explained the phenomenon this way: "An awful lot of children born in 2007 . . . have been competing with their parents' screens their whole lives."[2]

The same is true for our spouses. When we intentionally disconnect from our phones and make ourselves available to them at the end of a long day, we simply get to connect. No guessing, no stressing.

> *When our children have our intention, they don't need to get our attention.*

I love how Arlene Pellicane said it: "Think what would happen in your marriage if you reached out to touch your spouse as many times as you reached out to touch your phone."[3]

What would happen if you gave your loved ones your best instead of what's left? Hold fast as you fast and find out for yourself.

Dear Lord, I don't want to escape from stress or people anymore. During this fast, teach me to hold fast to You and to the people You've given me. It's hard to stay committed; please help me recommit. I want to put down the phone and touch my loved ones, to close my screen and open my arms. Bless my friendships and bless my family as I learn to bless them with my undivided attention in the days ahead. In Jesus's name, Amen.

DAY 4

Getting Social [IRL]

And let us consider how we may spur one another on toward love and good deeds, not giving up meeting together, as some are in the habit of doing, but encouraging one another—and all the more as you see the Day approaching.

Hebrews 10:24-25

I sat on my couch with Chanda as we talked about what she'd learned as she fasted from social media. She confessed, "The first couple of weeks were lonely. It's as though I had to learn all over again how to be social. My real-life friends didn't make it easy on me, either. I'd pick up my phone and call instead of text, but they wouldn't answer. Instead, they'd immediately send a text back: 'Hey, what's up?'"

Online, we use the acronym IRL. It stands for "in real life" and refers not to our online people but to those with whom we intimately do real life. Unfortunately, most of us have gotten so busy, with our heads down over our screens, we forget to look up and see the people right in our midst. At most we send texts or comment on one another's latest Instagram post. That's how "connected" we are—so connected online that we're disconnected in real life.

When social media becomes our native tongue, we're left tongue-tied and socially awkward IRL.

When social media becomes our native tongue, we're left tongue-tied and socially awkward IRL

Chanda and I weren't sitting alone. Twenty other women were crammed into my living room at the end of one of our annual sugar fasts. We had been fasting from sugar and feasting on God's sweet Word together. While we were part of an online community, we wanted to break our fast together, face-to-face. Over breakfast we took turns sharing what we had learned during our sugar-free days. That's when Chanda stunned us all. Shortly after beginning the sugar fast, she felt the Lord tell her to lay down social media too. While she loved cupcakes, she knew she was more distracted by Facebook. We were surprised at her gutsiness and leaned in to learn from her, because we sensed a similar pull in our own lives. A few days later many of us committed to begin a social media fast of our own.

Late that afternoon, I wrote out a list of things I said I valued but never seemed to have time for.

- Spend time with the Lord in His Word
- PRAY!
- Be present with the family
- Plan weekend fun
- Try new recipes
- Date my husband
- Read good books
- Clean the hall closet!

- Go for walks and stretch
- Get together with friends

This list became my checklist. These were the things I planned to do during my fast. I would "turn to" these things instead of social media.

When I have my phone in my hand and my laptop open on the kitchen table, I'm easily distracted. My priorities slip away. I don't have time for the things or people I value most. I'm tired too, so I leave my family to go to bed early, then spend an hour scrolling through other people's "togetherness" before falling asleep. I'm too busy getting nothing done to plan a date night or try a new recipe, and I'm certainly too busy to get together with friends.

Providentially, my friend Kathy sent me a text the very next morning, asking if I could meet up for a cup of tea. I had so much I needed to get done that day, but I remembered my goal to *get social* and decided not to wait until I had officially started the fast. "You bet," I texted back, and within an hour we were sitting across from one another at a coffe shop table. I left that date with a smile on my face. My intention of getting social during my upcoming social media fast was already influencing the way I was living my days. My time with Kathy confirmed that getting social beyond social media would have to become an important part of my life again, even after the fast.

While the primary purpose of fasting from social media is to replace online people with the person of Jesus Christ, it's also important to replace online people with real-life people. **The goal of fasting is always to lay down what is temporary and pick up what is eternal.** God is eternal, but so are His people. God created us as spiritual beings who would live forever in His presence. So when we take the time to invest in another person, we are sowing into what is eternal. Social media sometimes gives us a chance to connect and encourage, but more often we leave pithy comments and don't take the time to "encourage one another and build each other up" (1 Thess. 5:11). Though our days roll by in a ceaseless string of conversation, we don't usually converse.

A few days after that gathering at my home, I received an email from Beth, thanking me for the party and telling me she had thought of me that morning as she read her Bible. She quoted 1 Thessalonians 5:11 along with this verse: "And let us consider how we may spur one another on toward love and good deeds, not giving up meeting together, as some are in the habit of doing, but encouraging one another—and all the more as you see the Day approaching" (Heb. 10:24–25). The time together had been sweet, she said, and she wanted me to know she felt spurred on in both love and good deeds from having spent time in my home.

I was more determined than ever to redefine what "getting social" would look like during my social media fast. I wasn't merely getting my face out of Facebook in order to spend time face-to-face with God and my family; I wanted to intentionally say yes to those friends I had given up meeting with.

On the first day of my fast, I made a few phone calls to some IRL friends I'd been missing. "Want to go for a hike next Saturday morning?" I asked two girlfriends. "Bring the family over for dinner on Friday night!" I invited others. "How about a double date next week?" I asked a couple whom my husband and I hadn't seen in a while. Surprisingly, all three invitations were accepted. My first two weeks of fasting from social media freed up space in my social calendar to engage with people I had been too busy to see. All three of these times together with friends were richly edifying and so much fun.

The ones I love must never take a back seat to those I "like."

Since those first forty days, I have continued this holy habit of meeting together during my fast. In order to make my IRL relationships work, I keep my online relationships online and don't allow them to spill over into all the hours of all my days. I'm reminded of

Johann Wolfgang von Goethe's warning, "Things which matter most must never be at the mercy of things which matter least."[1] Christian fellowship with close, family-like friends must matter more than the constant chatter of hundreds or thousands of "friends" around the world. The ones I love must never take a back seat to those I "like."

Vulnerable lives aren't lived online. While we can be honest and authentic, even transparent, online, true vulnerability must be saved for the safe haven of close community, where we "carry each other's burdens, and in this way . . . fulfill the law of Christ" (Gal. 6:2). **It's hard to carry another's heavy burden with a phone in our hands.** When we empty our hands, we are able to carry furniture into moving vans, hold babies while new moms take showers, place casseroles in ovens, and grab hold of another's hands in prayer. Today, make a call and extend an invitation for some face-to-face fellowship with a friend you've been too busy for. It will be a blessing to both you and the one you reach out to!

Lord, I need to put down my phone and look up into the eyes of my friends. It's been a while, so it feels a little awkward. Give me the courage to invite people into my often-messy real life, where meals aren't photoshopped and curated for optimal Instagram likes. Help me to value what You value, Lord: the eternal souls of people. You're the best friend of all, so I ask this in Your name. Amen.

DAY 5

Grocery Stories

For we are his workmanship, created in Christ Jesus for good works, which God prepared beforehand, that we should walk in them.

Ephesians 2:10 ESV

When my children were very young, I walked them across the street to our local neighborhood park every morning. Sometimes we returned in the afternoon for one more push on the swing. With a preschooler, a toddler, and a baby, along with diapers, wipes, snacks, and sand toys, I had my hands full. I had a flip phone shoved into my overloaded diaper bag, though I never heard it ring. It was a point of contention in our marriage. "Why do you even have a phone?" my husband wondered. "You never answer it." The simple, obvious answer was that I didn't have a free hand with which to hold my phone. And I didn't keep it in my pocket because I didn't want to be distracted. The needs around me were too immediate.

Though I was busy interacting with my kids, I also discovered that the park had become my personal mission field. Sure, I was pushing my kids on swings and catching them at the end of the slide, wiping sand out of their mouths, correcting behavior, passing out snacks, and tossing a ball, but I was also talking with my neighbors.

Sometimes I'd bring my camera—the one that used actual film— and take pictures of my new friends with their children. A few days later I'd see these moms again and give them an envelope with half a dozen photos of them playing with their kids. Tearfully, they'd throw their arms around my neck, saying they didn't have any pictures of themselves with their children. Once my new friends felt good and loved, I'd invite them to join me for the mom's group at our local church, just two blocks down the street. On Thursday mornings a group of us would meet at the corner at 8:45, then push our strollers to Bethany Church. I can't imagine the conversations (or the harvest) I might have missed if I'd had a fancy smartphone in my hand.

Ephesians 2:10 tells us that God created us for good works He prepared beforehand for us to find and walk in. He didn't just make us for random good works. **He intentionally designed unique and specific good works for each of us and then gave us opportunities to serve and love in our homes, our local communities, and this great big world.** Every single day we are meant to be on a treasure hunt to find those good works.

Today, my boys are teenagers. We don't head to the local park like we used to, and I have a smartphone now. I'm connected to more people than ever before. However, I've found this constant connectedness doesn't just get in the way of my connection to God and my closest family and friends but also distracts me from the good works God planned for me to find beyond my front door.

In the beginning of this book I cited Matthew 22:36, where Jesus said that the most important commandment is to "'Love the Lord your God with all your heart and with all your soul and with all your mind.' This is the first and greatest commandment. And the second is like it: 'Love your neighbor as yourself.'" While I want to live simply, loving God and loving others, the reality is I'm often distracted—distracted by the busyness of life and by this age-old question: *Who are my neighbors?* Every time I ask the Lord, I immediately know His expansive, loving response. Our neighbors are everywhere, and they are everyone. Everyone you walk past today as you take your dog for a walk. Everyone you drive by as you pick up your children from school. Every person lined up for a latte at the coffee shop or using the coffee maker at work. Every person breathing the same air as you, even when you run into the grocery store for a few items.

Opening my phone closes me off to others, but closing my phone opens me up to those around me.

I've dreamed for years about writing a book entitled *Grocery Stories*. It would be a series of short stories chronicling all the miraculous interactions I've had at my neighborhood supermarket. The woman purchasing a few slices of turkey and a single serving of cranberry sauce at the deli counter on December 23, 2016, whom I ended up inviting to join my family for Christmas Eve dinner and church services. Or the lady I gave my freshly purchased bouquet of flowers to because she said, "Peonies are my favorite!" There was the man in the motorized chair who was trying to reach a packet of taco seasoning on the top shelf. And the butcher whose eyes filled with tears when I told him I believed God uses each of our hard days to teach us to trust Him more. Most memorable was the older woman who sat crying in the car next to mine, forehead on her steering wheel, fragile body shaking. I gently knocked on her window and asked if I could pray for her. She let me in her car and told me how her husband of fifty-some years had recently died. Shopping for one person always triggered her grief.

I used to always be on my phone as I ran in and out of stores, but then I wondered, *How many good works have I walked right by with my eyes on my phone? How many neighbors have I been too busy to listen to and love?* When we leave our phone at home, we're able to offer the world our undivided attention.

Can you imagine the parable of the good Samaritan being lived out today? Would we even see our neighbor, battered and bruised on the side of the road, let alone offer to help? I might have tripped over him myself, with my face in Facebook. Opening my phone closes me off to others, but closing my phone opens me up to those around me. I hope and pray that during these forty days you'll keep your phone in your purse or pocket so that you might live this life with empty, open hands—helping and serving and loving your neighbors. Not simply because you want to "be a good human," though that's a highly tweeted catchphrase in the world today. We want to be available to each appointed and anointed good work the Lord has prepared for us to walk in . . . daily!

> *Our phones, intended to connect us to people, become a barrier to the gospel when they are a barrier between us and others.*

Our phones, intended to connect us to people, become a barrier to the gospel when they are a barrier between us and others. Therefore, these forty days, let's actively, lovingly pursue the people in our paths. Each day is a treasure hunt! **Lift your eyes and find the good works God prepared for you to walk in today.**

Dear God, You made us to love You and to love others. You prepared us for good works and good conversations and good eye contact and generous smiles. You set us free to humbly interact with those around us, purposefully pursuing them just as you have patiently pursued us. Holy Spirit, give us the eyes to see those who are in need of our loving attention today. In Jesus's name, Amen.

Choose one!

Today I want you to think about just one of the many stores that you frequent. Can you picture a specific clerk behind the counter? Just one. How might you be a blessing to them the next time you shop there?

Now visualize one of your neighbors. How can you make yourself available to them? As you walk from your car to your house or sit outside while your children play in the front yard, recognize the mission field right in front of you, ripe and ready for harvest. Few people are called to plow and sow and reap on a global scale. But we are *all* called to the plot of land right in front of us.

> Then he said to his disciples, "The harvest is plentiful but the workers are few. Ask the Lord of the harvest, therefore, to send out workers into his harvest field." (Matt. 9:37–38)

Take a look at the harvest field right outside your front door and choose one person to intentionally engage with today.

DAY 6

A Few Good Friends

For where two or three gather in my name, there am I with them.

Matthew 18:20

I've never been popular by the world's standards. I'm not part of any "in" group; I've always felt more comfortable with a few close friends than many acquaintances. And, for the most part, I've been content with this. Don't get me wrong; junior high and high school were hard—that horrible but necessary season of life when everyone struggles to discover who they are and where they belong in this world. Except for that brief coming-of-age period, I've always been comfortable with myself. I'd even go so far as to claim Psalm 16:6: "The boundary lines have fallen for me in pleasant places."

However, even with my contented sensibilities, social media can take a toll on my feelings. Like most people, sometimes I come across pictures of "friends" getting together without me and feel the quick sting of rejection, and every now and again the sting stays with me for a few days. That's when I have to preach to my own heart what I know to be true: I don't need everyone to like me, love me, or invite me. As long as I am safe and secure in that most important, always-inclusive relationship with God through Christ, all other fellowship is merely icing on an already satisfying cake. Though I love frosting . . . this metaphorical cake doesn't need a ton of it. I'm loved. And so are you.

Being rooted in that love relationship allows us to bloom securely, even when we're tempted to feel insecure about our place in the virtual world. The truth is, we were never intended to be everyone's BFF.

> *We think we need thousands of "followers," but Jesus says we only need a couple.*

When Jesus speaks to us about friendship, He uses simple math. No big numbers, no hard equations. In Matthew 18:20, He tells us that in order to enjoy His presence, we just need a couple of close friends to enjoy Him with: "For where two or three gather in my name, there am I with them." In Ecclesiastes 4 we see again that we only need two or three people to help us up when we fall, to share a little body heat when we're cold, and to come to our defense when we're threatened. We think we need thousands of "followers," but Jesus says we only need a couple sincere friends. Though we send out "friend requests" like we're throwing around confetti, it's not necessary or even biblical.

> Two are better than one,
>   because they have a good return for their labor:
> If either of them falls down,
>   one can help the other up.
> But pity anyone who falls
>   and has no one to help them up.
> Also, if two lie down together, they will keep warm.
>   But how can one keep warm alone?

> Though one may be overpowered,
> two can defend themselves.
> A cord of three strands is not quickly broken. (Eccles. 4:9–12)

An intimate dinner party with a few friends around a family table is one of my favorite things in the world. I value time spent eating good food with dear people, friends who are willing to talk about matters that really matter. That's my kind of party, and those are my kind of people.

Years ago, my husband, Matt, and I moved to a new town and started attending a new church. After we got to know some people in an adult Sunday school class, I invited one of the families over for a pancake breakfast. We fed the children chocolate chip pancakes in the kitchen, then put a show on the family room TV for them. Around the dinner table, one room over, I brought out a spread of adult breakfast food. Halfway through our meal, Matt brought up a book he was reading, *Crazy Love* by Francis Chan. "It's challenging me so much," he said. "I've realized I don't love people as much as God's Word says that I should. The most convicting part is that I don't want to. For example, I don't invite people to stay at my house because they need a place to stay. I'd rather have people come visit who meet my needs for friendship rather than meet their need for shelter."

I'm not sure if Matt stopped to take another bite or just a breath. I don't know why he paused, but an awkward silence filled the dining room. Eventually, the other husband said, "Do you always talk about this sort of deep stuff?"

Not surprisingly, that couple did not become our closest friends. They never returned the invitation or had us around their family table. When a few families from that Sunday school class went on a camping trip, we weren't invited to pitch our tent beside theirs. I confess that it hurt at first, but I chose (and continue to choose) to believe that not everyone is meant to be my close friend. We'd talk with them at church as we stood in line to pick up our children from the nursery, but we never tried to go "deep" with them again.

It's okay to have surface-level relationships at church and online; not every post or conversation needs to evoke tears or incite joy. The challenge is striking a balance. **We live in a culture that values beautiful pictures but isn't comfortable with beautiful brokenness.** We can't value staying safe so much that we never venture below the surface into deeper waters with a few choice people.

Don't get me wrong; it's alright if your social media stream reads more like a personal scrapbook of highlights. It's a pictorial keepsake, an easy way to share the fun stuff with your extended family and friends. There's no shame in that. There's nothing wrong with a snapshot of your favorite food (#yum) and your date night (#lovehim) and trips to the park (#momlife). Hit "share" and watch the likes roll in, but consider yourself warned: don't get swept up in posting highlights for all to see and forsake the friends with whom you can safely share the lowlights. We all need a few trusted friends to come to with our private prayer requests, our fresh diagnoses, our confessions, and our fears.

Just the other day I received a group text from my friend Emily. She sent it to four of us, wishing one of our dearest friends, Summer, a happy forty-second birthday. For the next two hours we all joined in sending Summer birthday wishes, sharing pictures and updates about our families, and going deep with private prayer requests. One woman shared that she and her husband felt the Lord calling them to adopt through the local foster care system, another talked about her daughter's lack of friendships in the neighborhood and asked for prayer concerning a possible

> *Don't get swept up in posting highlights for all to see and forsake the friends with whom you can safely share the lowlights.*

move, and then Emily capped things off by saying, "I love this text string so much and I want to continue it regularly. You ladies introduced me to our Lord and Savior nearly twenty years ago. You will always be my heart sisters."

Heart sisters. For twenty years. In a world where we carry a thousand friends in our pockets and our purses, Emily has four she carries in her heart. Heart sisters.

We don't need everyone to like us, love us, invite us, or include us. In God's economy, two or three faithful friends make for great wealth. In the company of just a few, we get to experience the richness of His presence and the warmth of their sincere support. Let's ask God for contentment today.

Dear Lord, Thank You for giving me a couple of real friends. Though this digital age tempts me to believe I need the whole world (wide web) to like me, I really only need You and the small, intimate group of family and friends You've blessed me with. Thank You for the few gold strands You've carefully and graciously braided into the tapestry of my life. In Jesus's name, Amen.

DAY 7

Eyes on the Skies

The heavens declare the glory of God, and the sky above proclaims his handiwork.

Psalm 19:1 ESV

I was inside at the dining room table, writing out a grocery list, as my sons played in the pool in our backyard. The sound of their laughter wafted in through open windows. It was an unseasonably warm spring day—mid-March and already ninety degrees. Summer, it seemed, had come early to Southern California.

"Mom! Mom! Mom! Mom!" the boys called as they scrambled out of the water. I looked up to see what was causing the commotion and couldn't believe my eyes. Thousands of butterflies fluttered around the boys. Everywhere, as far as my eyes could see, butterflies swarmed and swirled in all directions. Immediately I ran toward my room. My first thought was to grab my phone. I needed to start a Facebook Live at once!

Halfway down the hall, I remembered I had just begun a forty-day social media fast. In addition to staying off of Twitter,

Facebook, and Instagram, I had decided to keep my phone in my room all day long so that I would be present and available to my family. But what was happening outside was amazing. I'd never seen anything like it in all my life. My thoughts swirled inside me as the butterflies swirled outside the window. I had a choice: share the spectacle with my online friends or soak it up with my family.

It was then that I remembered my mom's oft-repeated words: "Take a mental picture, Wendy." Whether I was roller skating along the ocean, barbecuing ribs on the grill with family friends, opening presents on Christmas morning, handing out daisies at church on Easter Sunday, or simply enjoying a peaceful Saturday afternoon planting pansies in the backyard, "Take a mental picture," she'd say. In other words, be all there. Commit the moment to memory. File away the sights and the sounds and the smells and the feelings. **When you engage all your senses, the memories remain long after pictures fade.**

Though my iPhone has a ridiculously impressive camera built into it, those photos only capture the visual display of God's glory. Take a video and you get to enjoy the sounds of laughter too. But live the moment, and the moment becomes a multisensory experience you'll cherish forever! As I walked out to the patio, the fluttering of butterfly wings brushed my skin. The slippery cool touch of my youngest son's arms around my middle made it hard to breathe, or maybe it was the miracle of the moment. I caught my breath, overwhelmed.

"There is a God!" I cried out to the boys.

"Good job, God!" my oldest shouted out loud.

We locked eyes then and smiled. He'd remembered how I taught him to define *praise* when he was just a toddler. "Praise is telling someone what a good job they did. It's the same with giving God praise. When you see something beautiful like a sunset or a newborn baby, simply tell Him, 'Good job, God!'"

"Good job, God!" we shouted together.

All three wet-from-the-pool boys were counting aloud, "178, 179, 180, 181, 182 . . ." I joined them in the counting, and we got to well over one thousand before the mass migration moved on. For the next few weeks, however, we saw at least twenty butterflies in any direction we looked everywhere we went throughout town.

Others had captured the moment on their cameras, but I caught the moment in real life—the whole glorious display.

Ann Voskamp regularly invites her readers to get outside and soak up the glory all around them: "If the whole

> *When you put down your phone, it's easier to lift up your eyes.*

earth is full of His glory, maybe our souls need a daily 'glory soak.'"[1] I couldn't agree more. Not just forty days a year, but three hundred and sixty-five. How do we do this on a regular basis with phones in our hands or our bodies hunkered down and hidden behind a computer monitor or TV? I don't know what it needs to look like for you, but here in my house, even when I'm not fasting, I'm keeping my phone plugged in to the charger in our bedroom for long stretches every day, and I'm getting outside to see what a good job God has done and to tell Him so.

When you put down your phone, it's easier to lift up your eyes. And when you lift up your eyes, you see not only your family and your friends, your neighbors, and the whole wide world full of people needing your loving attention but also the glorious display of a praiseworthy Creator. Every peach that grows in our backyard, with its thin velvet skin holding back the sweetest juice, is God's glory just waiting to be tasted. In every stream that runs cold over smooth stones, God's laughter can be heard. In every thunderclap, God's creation gives Him a rousing round of applause, inviting us to do the same.

Unfortunately for me, as soon as the skies begin declaring God's glory, I'm often posting a picture of it along with a time-consuming stream of hashtags: #psalm19 #theheavensdeclarethegloryofgod #declare #mastercraftsman #sunset #amazing #praise #glory #faithlife #creator . . . Sadly, during those sacred moments when my head is bowed over my phone, I miss seeing the setting sun transform the sky from mango to magenta as the Master Craftsman splashes heavenly hues across the canvas of heaven. Though those first moments sincerely stun me, I am quickly distracted from the celestial service in the sky by an overwhelming urge to post it online. And though I feel joy in sharing the image with my online friends, the truth is that I experienced only a few moments of glory when I could have soaked it up for another seven minutes. **In my attempt to share His glory with others, I often miss out on so much of it.** I miss much when I share much.

Years ago, I went on a famous hike in Yosemite National Park known as the Mist Trail. Afraid of damaging my phone, I left it with a friend who stayed behind with the youngest climbers. As the rest of us ascended the mountain beside the falls, we had to bend over and use our hands to prevent ourselves from slipping. The trail, hewn from massive slabs of granite, was slick with moss. A constant stream of waterfall droplets covered everything. At one point I looked over my shoulder and caught sight of the most vibrant rainbow. I couldn't stop myself. I stood right up and lifted my hands in response to the glory on display. The impulse to praise the Lord was too great! Strangers crawled past me on all fours while I stood erect, crying, with hands lifted high.

I miss much when I share much.

One of the men in our group yelled over the roar of the falls, "Wendy, get down now!"

It was dangerous for me to be standing on the slick, moss-covered slab of rock, but my whole being responded to the glory. It was foolish, but even more foolish is never looking up to see God's glory on display. Never looking up to the heavens, never

hearing the proclamation shouted night and day, day and night
. . . that's a whole other kind of slippery slope.

All the way down the mountain I repeated, "There is a God!
There is a God! The heavens declare it: there is a God!"

Good job, God! The rocks and the sunset and the skies cry out that You are marvelous! Help me to lay down my distractions so that I might lift up my eyes and lift up my praise! In Jesus's praiseworthy name, Amen.

DAY 8

Find the Apple

A word fitly spoken is like apples of gold in a setting of silver.

Proverbs 25:11 ESV

Recently, I found myself in the waiting room of a doctor's office, seated across from a mother and her child. The toddler played quietly on an iPad. The mother had her own phone out and was looking at something else. I spent the next moments flipping through my mental Rolodex of memories, remembering how hard it was when my kids were that age. They were always by my side or crawling up into my lap in lobbies like that one. Back then, I kept a bag of books and toys in our car specifically for waiting rooms and long car rides. Most of our books were *I Spy* books, with items hidden in colorful pages. Nestled together in waiting rooms, I would say things like, "Show me the apple," and my children would search the picture top to bottom, left to right, corner to corner, and then exclaim, "There it is!" With a pudgy finger pressed to the page, my boys would look up into my eyes, delighted to find me smiling back down.

Today, there's a different sort of Apple that our children long to spy. Before the age of two they know to search our purses and our pockets and grab it from our hands. They memorize our passwords before they can spell their names. We give it to them to keep them quiet in the car and still their wiggles at restaurants. We use it as a reward and take it away as a consequence, and I'm wondering if we have lost something precious in the process.

My goal isn't to shame us, whether we are parents, grandparents, or simply whiling away the hours in waiting rooms on our own. Instead, my hope is to remind us that we have the power to do hard things and make better choices about our phone use. **While it's more comfortable to keep ourselves occupied and our children quiet, we can keep our screens tucked away while we wait.** We can choose to look up and talk with strangers in waiting rooms or while waiting at a restaurant for our table. It may require self-control, but we can control ourselves. We can choose to not answer emails or return calls until we have a few moments alone. We can bring a book with us that engages our intellect and our imagination or choose to lift our eyes to the brightly colored pages of real life as we search for the apple (or the person or the conversation) hidden within it.

While our smart devices offer us an easy way to find anything in the world, they can also be a distraction from the things that can't be found

While our smart devices offer us an easy way to find anything in the world, they can also be a distraction from the things that can't be found with a Google search.

with a Google search. Things only discovered when we stay alert to life and those we're living it with. Love. Touch. Availability. Support. Opportunities to serve. Life lessons. A shoulder to cry on. A person to acknowledge. All apples of gold, all treasures to be treasured.

The wisest man in the world once wrote, "A word fitly spoken is like apples of gold in a setting of silver" (Prov. 25:11 ESV). King Solomon was full of wisdom, though he struggled to live it out. He wrote about self-control but lived like a glutton, out of control. The lesson for us is simple: knowing what's good and right, noble and true, excellent and praiseworthy, edifying and helpful isn't enough.

Let's camp out on this single proverb for the purpose of leaving these fasting days different from how we started them. We don't need more head knowledge (we can ask Siri for that); what we want is the wisdom to live it out. Take this verse to heart. As you set aside your digital Apples, search for settings of silver to place your golden apples. **How many words have remained unspoken because you were too distracted to engage with another flesh-and-blood human?** When I fast, I look up and find silver settings everywhere I go.

While shopping for a new dress, I see a woman on the other side of the display rack holding up a deep blue blouse. The color makes her eyes sparkle. It's the perfect shade for her, and I let her know. "That color is perfect for your eyes! You've got to try that on."

Don't forget that the apple on the back of your phone has a bite taken out of it—there is temptation at every turn.

As I'm making dinner, one of my kids walks by with earbuds in. I wave him down so he takes one plug out, then I say, "Put whatever you're playing on the house speakers so we can enjoy it together." The invitation was all he needed, and before long I'm listening to music I would never have chosen—but my son feels chosen—and that's an apple of gold shaking from the limbs of a silver tree.

Life is one big *I Spy* adventure when we're sitting in our heavenly Father's lap in the waiting room called life, looking for hidden apples in the pages of each new day.

While I pray you discover apples galore during your social media sabbatical, my hope is that you stay alert when you are back online. Don't forget that the apple on the back of your phone has a bite taken out of it—there is temptation at every turn. Keep your head up and your eyes lifted. Don't be like King Solomon, with wisdom in your head but a lack of wisdom in your life. That's not living at all. Practice this fully alive life now, so that you know how to keep on living when your fasting days are through.

Heavenly Father, I'm in Your lap now. You've opened my eyes to the storybook before us and I'm on the hunt for silver opportunities to place my golden apples. This is how I'm committed to live, spying out every good work and good conversation You have planned for me. I don't want to miss even one! In the good and golden name of Jesus, and for the glory of the Father, Amen.

DAY 9

Spring Cleaning

Cleanse me with hyssop, and I will be clean;
wash me, and I will be whiter than snow.

Psalm 51:7

Ten years ago, my mother-in-law, Paula, came to stay with her grandkids so I could accompany her son on a business trip to Europe. While our boys were at school during the day, she served me in an unforgettable way. She started with the pantry, taking everything out, wiping down the shelves, throwing away outdated groceries, and then organizing it all neatly. The next day she tackled the hallway closet, where craft supplies and sticker books had been shoved in beside board games and puzzles.

One afternoon, during the boys' karate class, she met a mom who asked her what she was doing with her time when the boys were busy. Paula told her about the pantry and hall closet, and the woman dropped her jaw. She was horrified that my mother-in-law had tossed nearly all of my seasonings, even if they had expired before my oldest child was born. Paula laughed uncomfortably and considered digging it all out of the trash can when she got back to the house. I'm glad she didn't.

Over the years, while I was chasing children and packing picnics for the park, my pantry and closets had become an overwhelming mess. My sweet mother-in-law wasn't trying to shame me but to bless me. And bless me she did! To this day, when I am overwhelmed by life, she offers to come watch the boys and clean my pantry. Sometimes I still say yes.

Each time I step back from the clutter of the online world, I'm amazed how much time is freed up to declutter my real world.

In recent years, however, I've learned to do more closet cleaning and pantry purging myself. This isn't simply because the kids are growing up, though that helps; the main reason I'm more productive is because I've freed up forty days each year by actively laying down my distractions. Each time I step back from the clutter of the online world, I'm amazed how much time is freed up to declutter my real world. As the Lord does a work in your heart, I hope you use some of your freed-up hours to bring some peace to your home. We can experience emotional peace when we bring order to the chaos of cabinets and cupboards. Drawers can be distracting when they're filled to overflowing. They're stuffed with too much stuff, and instead of getting rid of it, we cram more in. When it finally becomes too much, we're too busy to do anything about it because we've stuffed our lives too full too.

Is your closet a picture of how you consume what's online as well? More and more and more, as though more stuff brings more joy. I've come to discover, however, that less is more. Less time online. Fewer piles to weed through. Just as less distraction makes room for more devotion, less stuff makes room for more joy. Joy isn't found in our things; it's found in the presence of God.

> You make known to me the path of life;
> in your presence there is fullness of joy;
> at your right hand are pleasures forevermore.
> (Ps. 16:11 ESV)

I want to be careful with what I say, because decluttering isn't another thing to stack on your plate during your fast from social media. You don't have to clean out your fridge or organize the twelve boxes of Christmas decorations still stacked by the door. I am merely suggesting that you consider using some of these freed-up moments to free up some space in your real life. **The less you're owned by stuff, the more room you make for God.** And the more room you make for Him, the less you'll feel compelled to buy more fillers. Minimal stuff in your home equals maximum space for Him to make His home in you.

As you do some spring cleaning and decluttering during these fasting days, consider meditating on the cleansing work of Christ in your life. "Cleanliness is next to godliness" is often misquoted as a Bible verse,[1] but the Bible is clear that the only cleanliness that makes us right with God is the cleansing work He does in our lives. From the Old Testament through the New Testament, we are called to live clean lives *because we have been cleansed from all unrighteousness.* Try as we might, there is nothing we can do to clean up and make ourselves presentable to the King of Kings. Which is why the King sent His Son, Jesus Christ, to chase us down, clean us up, and bring us back to the Father.

Just as less distraction makes room for more devotion, less stuff makes room for more joy.

Ezekiel spoke God's prophetic words over a rebellious Israel long before Christ came to do the dirty work of our salvation. "I will sprinkle clean water on you, and you will be clean; I will cleanse you from all your impurities and from all your idols. . . . I will save you from all your uncleanness" (Ezek. 36:25, 29).

Years before that, another prophet came bearing a similar message. After King David's adulterous relationship with Bathsheba, the prophet Nathan came to David and confronted him about his sin. The Lord punished David by taking the life of his son. In the aftermath of his grief, David wrote:

> Have mercy on me, O God,
>   according to your unfailing love;
> according to your great compassion
>   blot out my transgressions.
> Wash away all my iniquity
>   and cleanse me from my sin.
> For I know my transgressions,
>   and my sin is always before me. . . .
> Cleanse me with hyssop, and I will be clean;
>   wash me, and I will be whiter than snow. . . .
> Create in me a pure heart, O God,
>   and renew a steadfast spirit within me. (Ps. 51:1–3, 7, 10)

Consider making this prayer your own. Is there any "stuff" you need to confess and throw away? Are you overwhelmed by the mess of sin hoarded inside your heart? Take it to the Lord. Allow Him to cleanse you by the washing of His blood. That's what He came to do. The blood He shed on Calvary is the cleansing spring, the ultimate "spring cleaning."

> Come now, let us reason together, says the LORD:
> though your sins are like scarlet,
>   they shall be as white as snow;

> though they are red like crimson,
> they shall become like wool. (Isa. 1:18 ESV)

My mother-in-law was so generous to roll up her sleeves and enter my mess. She cleaned out the hidden gunk that had been pushed into corners over the years. She didn't leave a crumb behind. She attacked my clutter with fervor and demonstrative love. I'll never forget that offering. Though it is a lovely memory, it pales in comparison to the cleansing work of Christ in me. **I pray that you use these days to tackle your messes head-on—not just those found in the hallway closet but also in the closet of your heart.** Open it up before the Lord and invite Him in.

> Create in me a pure heart, O God,
> and renew a steadfast spirit within me. (Ps. 51:10)

Dear Lord, The cleansing spring of Your blood is the spring cleaning I need most of all. I've been too distracted to tackle the mess in my closet, but I know You're more concerned with the mess in my heart. Cleanse me from all unrighteousness (1 John 1:9), save me from my uncleanness (Ezek. 36:29), and though my sins are scarlet, wash me white as snow (Isa. 1:18). I ask this in the cleansing name of Jesus, Amen.

DAY 10

Social Distancing

Let's walk right up to him and get what he is so ready
to give. Take the mercy, accept the help.

Hebrews 4:16 MSG

On Ash Wednesday, February 26, 2020, I logged off of social
media and silenced all other online notifications. I was
eager to step away from the online conversation and ready
to enjoy some undistracted time with my family. It had been a busy
year since my last social media fast. The kids were running multiple
directions five nights a week, and my husband and I barely had any
time together, just the two of us. While I knew that setting down
my phone would free up a little space in our jam-packed schedule,
I had no idea how much time together was coming our way.

Though I was aware of the COVID-19 virus and what was happening in China and Europe (and had even heard reports about
coronavirus cases in Washington state and a few other US cities),
I had no idea my social media fast would intersect with a global
social fast. Within three weeks, we were told to stay home until

further notice: schools closed, businesses shut their doors and furloughed their employees, sports seasons were canceled, city workers wrapped reams of yellow "warning" tape around park play structures, and churches closed their doors for Sunday services. Even as I write these words, we are still "sheltering at home." *Social distancing* is the term being used today.

People are responding to this forced time of isolation in different ways. Some have become paranoid, hoarding toilet paper and canned goods, afraid that resources will run out. Others are angry at politicians for not better preparing us for a potential pandemic. With the economy in a fragile place, many are frightened about their financial security. Parents and school administrators are hustling to help children get their online classes up and running. And we're all wearing masks and using hand sanitizer when we run to the store.

We've been told to not leave our homes unless there's something "essential" we need. Pharmacies, gas stations, and grocery stores are open for business, but that's about it. Everything else is considered nonessential—including getting together with friends. While some introverts around the world have never been happier, highly social extroverts have struggled. It makes me wonder how you're doing in the early days of this social (media) fast. If you're struggling, feeling out of touch, or missing the virtual touch of friends, you'll appreciate today's verse as much as I did when I came across it exactly ten days into my own literal lockdown. I felt as if God were saying to me, *Closer, come closer. Walk right up to Me and get what I'm so ready to give.*

While we may have been forced into social distancing during the COVID-19 pandemic, we intentionally chose to distance ourselves from our online relationships for these forty days. **Regardless of how we find ourselves in lonely seasons, I believe they are the perfect times to draw nearer to God than ever before.** He uses our loneliness to prick our hearts, get our attention, and invite us to seek His companionship.

Do you know how to do that? To seek Him and find Him (Jer. 29:13)? To draw near to Him and allow Him to draw near to you (James 4:8)? Do you understand what it means to "walk right up to God"? Or do you think this is all some sort of poetic metaphor? There's no better time to devote yourself to finding out and finding Him than during these lonely days. You're on a social media lockdown for the duration of this fast, so commit yourself to unlocking this mystery! Don't let yourself go through the motions of a digital detox and miss out on the nearness of the One you're fasting to find. If you want to learn to walk right up to God, start by considering how close He already is.

> *If you want to learn to walk right up to God, start by considering how close He already is.*

Psalm 139 communicates just how "with us" He always has been and always will be.

> For you created my inmost being;
>   you knit me together in my mother's womb.
> I praise you because I am fearfully and wonderfully
>   made;
>   your works are wonderful,
>   I know that full well.
> My frame was not hidden from you
>   when I was made in the secret place,
>   when I was woven together in the depths of the earth.
> Your eyes saw my unformed body;
>   all the days ordained for me were written in your book
>   before one of them came to be.
> How precious to me are your thoughts, God!
>   How vast is the sum of them!
> Were I to count them,
>   they would outnumber the grains of sand—
>   when I awake, I am still with you. (vv. 13–18)

Not only was God with you as your life was stitched together, He's been there ever since. Even now, He is still with you. Therefore, walking into His presence isn't as much about walking up to Him as it is about waking up to Him. "When I awake, I am still with you" (v. 18). Have you been asleep to His presence? Is now the time you get to finally wake up to the reality of His nearness? Or perhaps you get to reawaken after having been lulled to sleep by a sedentary existence in front of your screens? Wake up and find Him right there with you. In the absence of everyone else, He is there.

Walking into His presence isn't as much about walking up to Him as it is about waking up to Him.

During the start of the COVID-19 pandemic, we have been told to stay six feet apart from one another, but nothing restricts us from walking right up to the One who walks right up to us. While we stay away from one another in an effort to "flatten the bell curve" of the virus, the Prince of Peace is right there with us, ringing the bell as if to rouse us from our slumber. This time of social (media) distancing may be the wake-up call He's using in your life. You've silenced the bells and whistles on your phone. Can you hear Him call out to you now? *Wake up, look up, and walk up to Me. I'm right here, as close as ever.*

Closer-than-close Lord of Lords, Thank You for this season of social (media) distancing so that I can finally get social with You. You've been here all along. Now that I'm undistracted by everyone else's presence, I'm devoting myself entirely to Yours. I'm awake to Your nearness! In the up-close-and-personal, ever-present name of Jesus, Amen.

DAY 11

Get Your Phone off His Throne

Those who cling to worthless idols turn away from God's love for them.

Jonah 2:8

Eleven days ago you pressed pause when you stepped away from the constant chatter online. *Selah* is a Hebrew word, often used in poetry, that invites us to pause when we're reading the Bible. It can be translated as an emphatic "Amen!" but is often interpreted as "Wow. Give me a moment to think about that."

While *Selah* is used seventy-one times in the psalms, I would add a *Selah* after Jonah 2:8: "Those who cling to worthless idols turn away from God's love for them." In the quiet of a *Selah* pause, consider what it is that you turn to most. That which you turn to most often is often that which turns you away from God. *Selah.*

69

Authors Ruth Chou Simons and Troy Simons wrote, "What makes your heart beat fast will determine what your heart beats for. Be careful what you love."[1] If something other than God quickens your heart more than His love, take note. That which makes your heart beat fast may actually be the thing you need to fast from. While we may not be a culture that worships idols carved out of wood, many of us have made idols of our digital devices. During this forty-day fast, we are laying down our phones, physically turning away from the divisive distraction of social media and those we like in an effort to turn our attention back to the One we love. If you have made the subconscious choice to turn away from God's love over the years, you can make a conscious choice to turn back to it now.

That which you turn to most often is often that which turns you away from God.

In the days before my phone was smarter than I am, I had an acquaintance who owned a first-generation iPhone. While I had heard about smartphones, I'd never seen one or understood what made them so intelligent. Not only did this woman show me the wonders of her device but I recall vividly the way she jokingly referred to it as her boyfriend. Her husband laughed at the adulterous way she clung to it, always splitting her time and attention between her two loves. Though my phone at the time was a flip phone, I wasn't flip-flopping between my family and the rest of the world. I wasn't distracted then, but I am now. Most of us are. Which is why I'm asking the question, What divides your attention? That which divides your attention will divide your affection.

Since idolatry is an age-old problem that plagues us still, we must consider what else is sitting on the throne of our lives. Is it God or some other "god" that has a hold on us as we hold it? Two sovereigns cannot share a throne. "No one can serve two masters. Either you will hate the one and love the other, or you will be devoted to the one and despise the other. You cannot serve both" (Matt. 6:24).

What do you turn to most of all? Since you turn your face toward that which you love, then that which you face most is certainly that which you love most. **Eventually the thing you face the most (and love in equal measure) will rule your life.**

So, what do you face most? Name it. Name all of it. Write it in the margin of this book or in the pages of a journal. Perhaps your idol has nothing to do with social media. Perhaps it's constant snacking and nightly glasses of wine. Maybe it's your own comfort or the world's affirmation. Maybe working out and trying one diet and nutrition plan after the next get the majority of your attention. If the thought of laying down something in particular for forty days causes you immediate stress, you've likely found a false god vying for room on the throne of your heart.

I'm reminded of Isaiah 44:13–20, a passage that describes a carpenter who makes and bows down to false idols. He cuts down a tree and uses half of it to build a fire to keep warm and to cook a meal. With the other half he fashions an idol,

That which divides your attention will divide your affection.

to which he prays, "Save me! You are my god!" (v. 17). About this man, Isaiah says, "He feeds on ashes; a deluded heart has led him astray, and he cannot deliver himself or say, 'Is there not a lie in my right hand?'" (v. 20 ESV). Here's our takeaway: God created wood to be useful, but it's useless as a god. It's a lie if we think otherwise.

Can't we say that about anything and everything we cling to? Food is useful, but it's useless as a god. Money is useful, but it is useless if we rely upon it as our god. Phones are useful for staying connected at work, but they can't get the job done in terms of our salvation. Phones are useless at saving us and providing us with unconditional love and everlasting life. Only God can do those things. To think otherwise is to believe a lie.

It is good to lay down useful things for a season in order to remember that they are simply things to be used. **Even the most useful things go from useful to useless the moment we cling to them more than we should.** There is only one God, and He shares His throne with no other. Is your phone on His throne?

Name the things that are still distracting you from a devoted life, then lay them down. Turn from them and return to Him. Take some time to read Isaiah 44 in its entirety today. Notice how God is calling us back to Himself with these words:

> Remember these things, O Jacob,
>   and Israel, for you are my servant;
> I formed you; you are my servant;
>   O Israel, you will not be forgotten by me.
> I have blotted out your transgressions like a cloud
>   and your sins like mist;
> return to me, for I have redeemed you. (Isa. 44:21–22 ESV)

What an invitation! God alone provides abundant life (here and now) and eternal life too. Only God can redeem us. Free of charge. No monthly fees. No need to reset your password. The only password you ever need with Him is "yes and amen." Nothing else.

"Return to Me, for I have redeemed you." *Selah.*

Dear Lord, I am so sorry for having turned my face from Your love. I don't want my phone on Your throne any longer. I don't want anything else to take Your rightful place. Thank You, Lord, for the generous way You welcome me back each time I turn and return. In the only useful name in heaven and on earth, the only name that can save: Jesus. Amen.

DAY 12

Tech-Neck

Lift up your heads, O gates!
  And be lifted up, O ancient doors,
  that the King of glory may come in.
Who is this King of glory?
  The LORD, strong and mighty,
  the LORD, mighty in battle!
Lift up your heads, O gates!
  And lift them up, O ancient doors,
  that the King of glory may come in.
Who is this King of glory?
  The LORD of hosts,
  he is the King of glory! Selah.

Psalm 24:7–10 ESV

Pulling up to the front gate of the high school, I honked. Dozens of students looked up from their phones. My son was one of them. I could have just texted, "Look up!" but I was feeling snarky, so I gave a quick blast from the horn instead. Slightly embarrassed, he shook his head at me, slung his backpack over one shoulder and his lacrosse gear over the other, and came to the car.

For a split second I worried about my child's neck and wondered what the burden of books and bags was doing to his still-developing spine. I couldn't imagine that load was good for him. However, as I watched him trudging toward me, head back down, sending one more text before hopping in the car, I thought, *What long-term effects will this generation experience from spending so many hours in that head-down position every day?* Since then I've discovered that doctors are wondering the same thing. Recently, researchers labeled the condition of neck pain associated with device use as "text-neck" or "tech-neck."

A typical head weighs ten to twelve pounds and is intentionally designed to sit perfectly balanced upon the cervical spine. The neck's muscles, tendons, and ligaments all work together to keep the head upright, in a neutral position. Unfortunately, when we text, play video games, scroll through Instagram, or check our email, we drop our heads, hunch our shoulders, and jut out our chins, putting tension on our necks and backs.[1]

Bowing down for hours before our phones can cause more heartache than neck aches.

Hours each day are spent this way. That's why I wonder what the long-term physical effects will be. More than that however, I'm concerned about what it will do to us spiritually. Bowing down for hours before our phones can cause more heartache than neck aches. Yesterday we identified some of our false idols. We said no to the lie in our hands and lifted our gazes to the One True God. It's not enough to lay down our digital demigods—we must also look up in order to see Him. This has been the recurring theme of these early days of our fast.

> I lift up my eyes to the mountains—
> where does my help come from?

> My help comes from the LORD,
>   the Maker of heaven and earth. (Ps. 121:1–2)

We don't want to miss God's strength or His help, but most of all we don't want to miss out on HIM! Relationship with Him is available to us when we're on the lookout. When we sit with our heads down for too long, however, it's possible to fall back asleep literally and figuratively—physically and spiritually! But remember our lesson from two days ago: God's calling us to walk up to Him by waking up to Him and staying awake to Him.

I love how *The Message* interprets Psalm 24:7–10:

> Wake up, you sleepyhead city!
> Wake up, you sleepyhead people!
>   King-Glory is ready to enter.
>
> Who is this King-Glory?
>   GOD, armed
>   and battle-ready.
>
> Wake up, you sleepyhead city!
> Wake up, you sleepyhead people!
>   King-Glory is ready to enter.
>
> Who is this King-Glory?
>   GOD-of-the-Angel-Armies:
>   he is King-Glory.

Let's lift our heads, our sleepy heads. How awesome that the God of angel armies wants to come into our personal kingdoms and bring His kingdom to life in us! That's why we're told to "lift up your heads, O gates!" (v. 7 ESV). A gate is the entrance to one's kingdom, one's city, one's home, one's most intimate abiding place. I've heard it said, "The eyes are the windows to the soul," but I believe the Bible is telling us that our eyes are not windows but gates. God isn't timidly tossing pebbles at our windows. He isn't sneaky like that. He has always been about coming through the doors of our lives.

In Matthew 24, Jesus encouraged His followers to keep their eyes open, ready for His return. He said that the time of His return was "right at the door" (v. 33). Oh yes, let's keep our doors wide open, ready and waiting to receive Him!

That said, I know we're all going to see Him when He does come back, eyes lifted or not. Jesus said, "For as lightning that comes from the east is visible even in the west, so will be the coming of the Son of Man" (Matt. 24:27). While I believe He wants our eyes on the skies, anticipating His return, living like He could be coming today, even those fast asleep are going to see Him descend with a shout. In that moment we're all going to bow. Not dropping our heads over phones but dropping to our knees. Every knee will bow before Him, those who were found ready and waiting and those who were sleepwalking through their days, unprepared.

Though I'm attempting to make a case for us to lay down our phones and lift our eyes in anticipation, it's possible that God will use this digital age to fulfill this prophecy. Perhaps Jesus's coming will be large enough for everyone to see at once, or maybe we will all get to witness the second coming via livestream! Jesus will be larger than life, I imagine, with His feet planted firmly on the Mount of Olives, but maybe we'll see it over Facebook Live! I don't know how His return is going to happen, but I know that it will.

If and when you bow your head, make sure it's because you're praying.

In the meantime, let's lift our "gates" to welcome His kingdom into our own little kingdoms. Practically speaking, that's what we're doing these forty days. We're standing tall with eyes open and hearts open too. Christ is coming back for His church. Let's not be found sleeping over our tables or tablets. Lift your head and lift your eyes!

Today, let me challenge you to engage your core muscles and stand up taller than you have in years. Imagine a balloon tied to the top of your head. Let your head float up, elongating and straightening your "tech-neck." Roll back your shoulders and take a deep breath. Your body is aligned now, but we want to be spiritually aligned too. Open your spiritual eyes and lift them to the mountains. If and when you bow your head, make sure it's because you're praying.

Dear Lord, I don't want to drop my head and lower my eyes and miss out on Your power or presence in my life. You are where my help and my hope come from. You're inviting me, as You have invited everyone over the centuries, to open my heart to You now. Thank You for the way You continue to pursue me, desire to indwell me, and radically transform me.
I love You, God of angel armies! Amen.

DAY 13

Golden Nuggets

The law of the LORD is perfect,
   refreshing the soul.
The statutes of the LORD are trustworthy,
   making wise the simple.
The precepts of the LORD are right,
   giving joy to the heart.
The commands of the LORD are radiant,
giving light to the eyes.
The fear of the LORD is pure,
   enduring forever.
The decrees of the LORD are firm,
   and all of them are righteous.
They are more precious than gold,
   than much pure gold;
they are sweeter than honey,
   than honey from the honeycomb.

Psalm 19:7–10

My youngest son learned a wonderful skill from his second grade teacher, Mrs. Carney. That sweet woman told Asher that when he's reading the Bible, he's actually mining for gold. Pure gold. She placed a golden highlighter in his hand and told him to find the golden nuggets that God wants him to apply to his life, verses that speak to his heart and seem most important to him personally.

Over the course of his young life, Asher had seen me do the same: interacting with God in His Word by taking out my highlighter, underlining Scriptures, writing in the margins, or leaving the date and a prayer beside a meaningful passage that resonates in some new way. At the end of that school year, my son took all the money he had saved and bought a journaling Bible just like mine—one with wide margins to write those golden nuggets out in his own words. Five years later he's still working his way through, with a golden highlighter in his hand.

Just last weekend he walked into my room and found me in bed, at it again. My knees were up with the Bible propped against them. A pen and a highlighter were cradled in my lap. He flopped down beside me and said, "I read my Bible this morning too."

Looking up at my eleven-year-old, I smiled and then asked, "Any golden nuggets?"

Asher took a moment to remember, then said, "I don't know if I'll quote it right, but it's about not being ashamed of God or the gospel." I turned a few pages and found the verse he was referring to in the opening chapter of Romans. When I pointed to the passage, he saw that I had highlighted it myself at one point. On another day I had underlined it too. And then, with a different pen, which made me think I must have written it during a third time through the same passage, I had added a prayer asking the Lord for more courage. Asher read my prayer and nodded his amen, then read the verse aloud: "For I am not ashamed of the gospel, because it is the power of God that brings salvation to everyone who believes: first to the Jew, then to the Gentile" (Rom. 1:16).

My boy smiled once more, kissed my face with his thin lips, and left me alone to dig for more gold. I turned to Psalm 19 and read,

> The decrees of the LORD are firm,
>   and all of them are righteous.
> They are more precious than gold,
>   than much pure gold. (Ps. 19:9–10)

Next, I picked up *The Message* from my bedside table and turned to Psalm 119. Though I don't read from this particular version as much as I do some others, glimmering flecks of gold reflected up from its pages nonetheless. I'd been here before and was back again, searching for more treasure. I found it in verse 72:

> Truth from your mouth means more to me
>   than striking it rich in a gold mine.

Sometimes I get myself into a bad place with social media, scrolling habitually through the same posts I'd looked at twenty-three minutes before—as though I'm going to "strike it rich" and discover something new, something of worth I didn't see the last time I thumbed through the same feed. **When I put down my phone and pick up my Bible, however, I discover again that God's Word is always fresh.** There's always something new for me there when I'm weary and wanting or just plain bored.

Though the words are the same, new revelation springs up from the ancient text each time I open it up. Pure gold. I highlight it the first time, underline it my next time through, circle a word and jot down the definition of the Greek translation when I'm sitting in church, and sometimes scribble a prayer in the margin along with the date. No matter how many times I revisit the same verses, they are always 24-karat gold. And this precious metal can be passed down to future generations! Unlike the hours spent snapchatting or binge-watching HGTV, time spent with the Lord in His gold mine yields a return that can be passed down as an inheritance to our sons and daughters and their sons and daughters for a thousand generations!

My mother's father was a Baptist minister in the Midwest. Throughout the week he went mining for gold, as ministers of the gospel are known to do, so that on Sunday morning he could stand in the pulpit, open the Scriptures, and share the wealth he'd unearthed. Though he died right before my second birthday, I like to think he passed down to me his love for discovering and sharing the riches of God's Word. Providentially, my grandpa had taken some of his savings to buy me a half-ounce gold coin to celebrate my birth. How meaningful that coin is to me today.

When I put down my phone and pick up my Bible, I discover again that God's Word is always fresh.

What treasure do you spend your day digging for and living for? Do you return again and again to the always fresh, precious, relevant, and applicable Word of God? Or do you mindlessly turn and return to the same old social media feeds and online games? Do you look incessantly at your LinkedIn account, eager to see if someone new has looked you up—or do you look up?

There are times that social media points me to God's Word. Absolutely! And honestly, that's my reason for posting most of the time. Though sometimes I share family photos, my main desire is to use social media as a virtual pulpit from which I can share the gold I've found and teach others how to dig into God's Word for themselves.

Social media, however, is not the gold mine. It is not what we turn to for our riches. It's simply a display case where we all get to share what we have mined that day (whether from the world or from the Word). If you follow wise people who love God and others well, then you'll likely be encouraged by them. If you follow friends who love to hike and always have a camera slung over their shoulder, their feed may feel like *National Geographic*. Either way, you don't need to scroll past the same post twenty-three times. God's Word, however, should call us back repeatedly! There's more to discover, first with your highlighter and then with your pen, leaving notes for yourself to read again the next time you pass through that same passage.

How many times do you open various apps each day, looking for something new? **Perhaps you're mining for the wrong riches in the wrong mine.** Or maybe you place too high a value on connecting with others. Ask the Lord to speak to you about what it is you are looking for and where you might find the treasure you need most of all.

God's Word is more precious than gold. Turn to it repeatedly.

God's Word is more precious than gold. Turn to it repeatedly. Find and apply those golden nuggets in your own life, first and foremost. And then, perhaps, you'll be able to share them with your friends online.

Oh Lord, Your Word is pure gold. Always has been, always will be. Each time I open it, I find that it's as good, if not better, than it was the time before. Forgive me for opening up my laptop and my phone apps more than I open up Your Word. I need Your wisdom more than I need the world's pictures and posts. Undistracted, I'm eager to grow in devotion now. Thank You for calling me back to the deep and rich mine of Your loving communication!

In the precious-as-gold name of Jesus, Amen.

Read Your Bible

I love leading you through a verse or two each day, but it is my hope that you are actually opening your Bible and digging into it for yourself. **These short chapters were meant to whet your appetite, not satisfy your hunger.** Are you opening up your Bible during these fasting days? Limiting or eliminating social media may help, but the ultimate goal isn't less social media but more time spent getting social with Jesus. Get social with Jesus as you meet with Him in His Word.

Author Alisha Illian summed it up like this: "Read your Bible. You can eat all the kale, buy all the things, lift all the weights, take all the trips, trash all that doesn't spark joy, wash your face and hustle like mad, but if you don't rest your soul in Jesus you'll never find your peace and purpose."[1]

Open up your Bible today, look up today's verses, read them in context, and find that peace and purpose for yourself.

DAY 14

Stop Scrolling, Start Strolling

He has told you, O man, what is good;
and what does the Lord require of you
but to do justice, and to love kindness,
and to walk humbly with your God?

Micah 6:8 ESV

The first time I stepped away from social media, I lost more weight than I usually do while fasting from sugar. I was shocked, but the more I thought about it, the more sense it made. After all, I wasn't sitting down for hours on end. I was up and moving. As I moved, my heart would have already been pumping, blood already flowing even when not moving, and my body burning fat. and my body was burning fat. My metabolism woke up and my emotions did too. Physically I felt good, but emotionally I felt even better because my body was cranking out feel-good endorphins. Sitting on the couch, slumped over my phone,

84

I depended on comments to make me feel good. I've discovered, however, that moving makes me feel better. **Strolling makes me feel better than scrolling ever could.**

I've always known that movement is crucial for our physical, mental, and emotional health, but I didn't know how good it was for me spiritually until I fasted from social media. Perhaps it has something to do with the fact that we can't spell *movement* without these two words: *Move me.* Movement is like a physical prayer, inviting the Lord to move us on the inside.

There are seasons in my life when I get into unhealthy, sedentary places both physically and spiritually. I get stuck and I need God to move me out of that stagnant life. While fasting brings me to my knees, before long the Holy Spirit lifts me to my feet and gets me up and moving. Every time I fast from my phone, I experience this holy lifting followed by the Spirit's shove.

The first time I fasted from social media, I noticed that in lieu of scrolling I started strolling—and not just going on walks but walking with God. Instead of sitting for hours (snap)chatting with friends, I started walking and chatting with Him. He became my walking buddy in a way I hadn't experienced in a long time. As we walked and talked, I recognized we were growing our friendship— a friendship I had wanted to invest in but was always too busy or too tired for. Fasting freed up the time and energy I needed to get moving, and as my body got stronger, my friendship with God did too.

As we prepared to launch this book, the publisher sent me a potential book cover. It was absolutely beautiful! A gorgeous chair upholstered in green fabric embroidered with enormous pink flowers sat beside a stack of antiquated books with a steaming cup of tea balanced on top. The whole scene was lovely and inviting. I wanted to sit and make myself comfortable, but something about the cover was wrong. I realized what the problem was: that serene scene didn't tell the story of my fasting days. When I fast from social media, I don't just sit with God for a few quiet moments in the morning; I spend all day with Him, on the move.

I suggested instead an image of a woman fully awake and eager for the day ahead. I wanted her hands and her body (maybe even the tilt of her head) to shout, "I'm ready, God! I don't want to miss a moment of what You've planned for me today."

You are now two weeks into your fast. I hope you're waking up more energized and expectant with each passing day, stretching your arms open wide like the woman on the cover of this book, head up and eager for the day and the Day Maker. Use your empty hands to grab more than a few moments with Him; spend all day by His side.

Don't just spend a little time with Jesus today; spend today with Jesus!

How about it? Don't just spend a little time with Jesus today; spend today with Jesus! You have the time and energy to do that now. Go for a literal walk with Him. I'm reminded of these lyrics to the old sacred song "In the Garden."

> I come to the garden alone,
> While the dew is still on the roses,
> And the voice I hear falling on my ear
> The Son of God discloses.
> And He walks with me,
> And He talks with me,
> And He tells me I am His own;
> And the joy we share as we tarry there,
> None other has ever known.[1]

Oh, to hear our Savior's voice calling us out for a walk, that He might talk with us as with a friend. Such was the case with Enoch.

The Bible tells us that Enoch lived in close companionship with God. Not only did he enjoy God's fellowship for over three hundred years, but the Bible seems to say Enoch actually stepped into a forever-fellowship with God at the end of his life on earth. There's no mention of his death. See for yourself in Genesis 5:23–24: "Altogether, Enoch lived a total of 365 years. Enoch walked faithfully with God; then he was no more, because God took him away."

I love the idea of Enoch taking one seamless step into the eternal kingdom of the One with whom he walked on earth, and I believe that same forever friendship is available for us all to enjoy. Though our time on earth will come to an end, our time with God will continue. We are spiritual beings encased in flesh. When that flesh wears out, our spirits are just getting started. Like Enoch, we can walk with God during our lives here, and then, one day, we can find ourselves walking with Him in His heavenly kingdom. Amazing! His presence in our lives never skips a beat or a step. His nearness never wanes; His companionship never ends. The relationship we begin here continues there.

While I loved the image on that first potential book cover, a short time sitting in a chair with God isn't what I need most. I've got to learn to remain with Him all day long, because our unending fellowship won't ever cease. The New American Standard Bible translation of 1 Thessalonians 5:17 tells us to pray without ceasing. To do that, we've got to stay close to God—no matter what we're doing or where we're going. Ceaseless prayer doesn't require us to cease walking but to learn to talk as we walk.

Ceaseless prayer doesn't require us to cease walking but to learn to talk as we walk.

God has told us clearly that He wants us to walk with Him: "He has shown you, O mortal, what is good. And what does the LORD require of you? To act justly and to love mercy and to walk humbly with your God" (Mic. 6:8). Of course, it's hard to walk humbly with God if you aren't walking with Him at all. And it's impossible to stroll when you incessantly scroll. Since you've taken a break from scrolling with your thumbs, now's the time to start moving your feet.

Amos 3:3 asks, "Do two walk together unless they have agreed to do so?" God, through the presence of the Holy Spirit, is eager to have you join Him today. Won't you agree to meet Him? Don't simply give God a few minutes in the morning; give Him your whole day. **Practice the presence of God continually, because friendship with God continues.** One day we're going to take our final step here and start our adventure with Him there. That's why we need to spend more time strolling than scrolling!

Dear Lord, Thank You for inviting me to spend time with You today. Not just a little bit of time, but all of my time. No matter what I'm doing or where I'm going, You're with me. I choose to walk with You and talk with You, now and forever. In Jesus's energizing name, Amen.

DAY 15

Fill My Cup, Lord

Then Jesus said to his disciples, "Whoever wants to be my disciple must deny themselves and take up their cross and follow me."

Matthew 16:24

I have an early memory of my mom sitting at the piano in our family room, singing the hymns she sang as a child. She knew them by heart and now I do too. The first verse to "Fill My Cup, Lord" is embedded in my memory: "I was seeking for things that could not satisfy. . . . I heard my Savior speaking—'Draw from My well that never shall run dry.'"[1]

I am so grateful the words of that song have remained in my heart all these years, but I am even more grateful for the Bible story that inspired its lyrics. In John 4, Jesus encounters a Samaritan woman who went to the community well to draw water in the middle of the day. Surely, no one else would be there, since every other woman fetched her day's water long before the sun was high in the sky. This woman, however, went when she was sure to be alone. She had lived with multiple men over the course of her life and had a poor reputation, so she snuck around, shamed and ashamed, avoiding the other women in town. But when she arrived at the well on this day, she found she was not alone. Jesus was there.

I love the minor detail in this story that tells us Jesus had sent His disciples into town to get some food. We know from other stories that Jesus could have fed His followers in some miraculous way, turning stones into bread, and yet this time He didn't. While the disciples were physically hungry, Jesus knew this woman had a deep spiritual hunger that normal food or drink could never satisfy. So He sent His disciples away, knowing she might not open up to Him if a mob of men were around. Jesus didn't want anything or anyone to distract her from the devotion that was about to flood her heart from the inside.

He asked this unnamed woman to give Him a drink of water from the well. Surprised that a Jewish man would address a Samaritan woman, she asked Him why He was talking with her. Jesus told her that if she only knew who He was, she would be asking Him for a drink, and He would give her living water—a drink that would leave her fully satisfied, finally.

Confused at such a ridiculous notion, the woman asked, "How would you draw water without even a bucket?"

Gently and patiently, Jesus responded, "Everyone who drinks this water will be thirsty again, but whoever drinks the water I give them will never thirst. Indeed, the water I give them will become in them a spring of water welling up to eternal life" (John 4:13–14).

Immediately, the woman begged for this drink. If she could have some eternally satisfying water, she wouldn't have to keep coming back to this old well. She could hide forever and avoid the embarrassment of being seen. She could hide away with her sins and never leave the house. **But Jesus didn't want to fill her up so that she could remain in her sin; He wanted her to be free from sin.** That's what He, the Water of Life, is for. He removes sin.

According to Levitical law, many things could make a person unclean, but the only way an unclean person could be made clean again was through a purification ritual. This often involved a cleansing bath. The ritual symbolized the washing away of sin. Everyone who lived around the Jews knew this tradition, even the Samaritan woman. However, when Jesus the Messiah came to earth, He came to clean us up Himself.

Jesus wasn't offering to take away this woman's literal thirst for water. He was talking about His ability to cleanse her from her sins and satisfy the deep, misplaced thirst that drove her to make those sinful choices in the first place. Jesus claimed to be the source of her cleansing and completing. One believing drink from the Savior, and a cleansing fountain of forgiveness and salvation would bubble up from deep inside her and fill her.

Jesus told the woman to go get her husband so that he could have some of His water too. When she confessed to having no husband, Jesus said, "The fact is, you have had five husbands, and the man you now have is not your husband" (v. 18).

Shocked, the woman knew that no ordinary stranger could have known her intimate and hidden sins. When Jesus told her He was the Messiah, she dropped her water jug and ran to tell everyone in town. Every person she had previously tried to avoid, she went to find. "Come, see a man who told me everything I ever did. Could this be the Messiah?" (v. 29). She invited them to come find out for themselves. In an instant she went from hiding to publicly professing her hope in God. If you've ever had sin in your life and then encountered the Messiah for yourself, you know the incredible relief hope brings. I've experienced it too.

> *We're always looking but never finding—until we find the One who came looking for us.*

Though I've only had one husband, I am the woman who met Jesus at the well. I think to some degree she represents us all. Whether we've attempted to fill the void with work or wine, men or media, phones or food, nicotine or new clothes, we've all turned to things to quench the ache and kill the pain, to tell us we're worthy, or to meet some other deep need. Except they never do, which is why we keep cramming more in. We're always hungry but never satisfied, always thirsty but never quenched. **We're always looking but never finding—until we find the One who came looking for us.** Just as He came looking for the woman at the well, Jesus came looking for us. He chased us down in our sin and then poured Himself out as a drink offering: "Ask *Me* for a drink and you'll never thirst again."

Goodness, what a promise! Perhaps the story of the woman at the well is your story too. Maybe you've tried it all and are finally ready to see if this Jesus is true to His Word. Or maybe you're still sneaking to the well at midday, avoiding the critical eyes of your family and friends because everyone knows your appetite is insatiable and your lifestyle self-destructive. Accept the only drink that can both cleanse and satisfy you in one gulp.

The Living Water who cleanses us from all our unrighteousness also satisfies that insatiable hunger that got us into trouble in the first place.

I don't know what you've been running to in a mad pursuit to find love, desperate for affirmation and needing to feel safe and secure and all filled up. But nothing and no one will ever be able to meet that need—apart from Jesus. The Living Water who cleanses us from all our unrighteousness also satisfies that insatiable hunger that got us into trouble in the first place. Have you asked Jesus for a drink?

My fasting friend, if you have never come to Jesus by faith and accepted the forgiveness and cleansing He offers free of charge, the invitation is yours. Pray with me now:

Jesus, Nothing else has worked to cleanse me from sin or get me to stop sinning. There's nothing I can do on my own to get right with God either. I need You. I need a drink of what You offer. I'm ready to accept it. I want to do that now. I accept that You came to save me from my sin. And I believe You took the punishment I deserve. You didn't just die for me either. You rose again, proclaiming victory over my ongoing struggles. Count me in! I want what You're serving: living water, that I might never drink from the wrong well again.

In the saving, satisfying name of Jesus, I believe. Amen.

DAY 16

Well?

My people have committed two sins:
They have forsaken me,
   the spring of living water,
and have dug their own cisterns,
   broken cisterns that cannot hold water.

Jeremiah 2:13

*S*ometimes when I speak at church events, I feel a little uneasy. I know people see me standing on the stage and assume I don't know the inner turmoil and deep soul-sadness they harbor inside. They think I have it all together, that I've always drunk deeply from the well of living water. They don't know about all the empty cisterns I dug before I met Jesus at the same well where He met the Samaritan woman. They don't know my story. They don't realize that all God's people share some variation of the same story.

In Jeremiah 2:13, the Lord stated emphatically that His people "committed two sins." First, they abandoned Him, the spring of living water. Second, they dug a new well, a broken well, an inefficient cistern that couldn't even hold water. No verse in this entire book sums up our relationship with God and our relationship with the world better than this one. We turn from the well of His overflowing love and dig like crazy, hoping to hit a water source of affirmation. All our effort gets us nowhere. We're thirstier than ever when we spend our days gulping from the wrong source.

That was my story. Today when I speak to women's groups about fasting and addiction and the wellspring of God's satisfying love, I share a poem I wrote that includes these words:

We're thirstier than ever when we spend our days gulping from the wrong source.

> Well . . .
> I tried it all,
> Blamed the fall
> Life was hard
> That's all.
> Consumed and tried
> To satisfy
> Pushed stuff and food and men inside
> That vacuous chasm,
> Which made my life spasm,
> I couldn't fathom
> Enough passion to make me feel loved.
>
> Well . . .
> Nothing worked, not for long.
> Maybe the length of a song,
> The perfect love song
> In a country bar, two-steppin' to George Straight
> Moving circles with a man who wasn't even my date.
> But oooh, for the length of that song . . .
> I knew it felt wrong.
> Looking for love in all the wrong places
> Tangled embraces.

Well . . .
You might like to know just how
Just how I'm standing here now.
A bunch of church ladies
Listening to me,
like I've got the corner on Christianity
purity
religiosity!
But technically, logistically.
All I did was take the outstretched, nail-scarred hand
of the One who took my heart to therapy.
Who handed me . . .
A cool refreshing drink of living water.

What about you? What's your story? Can you pinpoint where you've turned over the years to satisfy your thirst and meet your deepest needs? *Do you even recognize what your deepest needs are?* Some dig their wells in the land of social media because they want validation; others dig at work because they need success to feel secure. Many people even dig deep wells at church, serving and digging and digging and serving because they think their worth is tied up in their reputation as a servant. We're all endlessly digging, until we discover that no man-made well holds one single drop of life-giving water.

Well? What about you?

If you can pinpoint the broken cisterns you've dug over the years—and why—there's hope you can turn from them and turn to Him. In the early pages and early days of this fast, we lifted our eyes from our screens. So often we look to our screens in an effort to be seen, but my hope is that you're starting to understand just how satisfyingly seen you already are, and how safe and secure you already are. **When the fount of that precious knowledge starts bubbling up in you, an endless stream of refreshment and restoration will heal your hurts and transform your life!**

When you look up from all the useless cisterns you've dug, you will find Him—truly find Him—there. And you will abandon the broken cisterns that never worked to heal your brokenness.

We're all endlessly digging, until we discover that no man-made well holds one single drop of life-giving water.

So often our wounds lead us to drink from the wrong water. A woman who was verbally or sexually abused ends up needing the constant attention of abusive love. The man who was only recognized by his father when he did something praiseworthy digs deep wells at work in hopes of getting another round of applause. Those who have only been valued for their looks or their selfless acts of service keep digging and digging and digging. Our wounds drive us to wrong waters, but Christ's wounds heal the brokenness in us that broken cisterns can never touch. He's the only way to be satisfied.

Open up the wellspring of God's Word today, read Jeremiah 2:13, and use your highlighter on it because this one is pure gold. We've struck it rich; there's an endless supply of affirming and healing and satisfying living water available to us when we turn and return to it.

Speaking of turning, turn a few more pages in your Bible and find Jeremiah 29:11–14.

"For I know the plans I have for you," declares the LORD, "plans to prosper you and not to harm you, plans to give you hope and a future. Then you will call on me and come and pray to me, and I will listen to you. You will seek me and find me when you seek me with all your heart. I will be found by you," declares the LORD, "and will bring you back from captivity."

If you've been digging your own deep cistern in hopes of meeting your deepest needs, this promise is for you. I know I gave you this invitation yesterday, but I feel led to extend it again today. If you haven't turned or returned to the Lord's love—if you're still held captive by the likes of this world—lay down your shovel and dive into the deep and deeply healing waters of God's eternal love. There's nothing you've done to deserve it and nothing you need to do but accept it.

Dear Lord, Your invitation is like Your well, boundless and never-ending. Thank You for calling me to Yourself. Thank You for helping me to see why I've gone astray. Please heal my wounds as I put my full attention on Yours. My wounds keep me wounded, but Your wounds bring the healing I've been looking for. I'm diving in to Your generous well, because mine simply hasn't been able to get the job done! In Jesus's name, Amen.

DAY 17

Chosen

Therefore, as God's chosen people, holy and dearly loved, clothe yourselves with compassion, kindness, humility, gentleness and patience.

Colossians 3:12

I f I could sum up with one word the powerful pull of social media, I'd start with *wanted*. We desire to be wanted, liked, and loved. Perhaps it began in elementary school when pretty children gathered around pretty lunch boxes, trading fruit roll-ups for chocolate pudding cups. Those carrying brown bags and bologna sandwiches felt on the fringe of acceptance even then.

Accepted. Maybe that's a better word. Our desire to be accepted grew as we grew. Parties, pimples, and popularity collided in a mass of hormonal humanity during junior and senior high school. We grew out of the lunch box phase into the awkward adolescent stage. Each invitation to pull up a chair or join a group of friends for a movie affirmed us and approved us.

Approved. The word *approval* also sums up the pull of social media. We longed for approval back then, and we strive for it now.

Perhaps we didn't know how much we needed approval when we opened our social media accounts, but over time we started shaping our sharing so that others might like, want, affirm, invite, and approve of us. Every time we publish a post, we're asking those same cool kids: Do you approve of my sense of humor? Do you think I'm witty? What about my children? Do you approve of my family? Look how much I've grown up! If they like our posts, they just might like us. The thumbs-up icon is our approval-o-meter. Other people's approval feeds our self-approval, and maybe that's what we're lacking most of all.

I've fasted from sugar enough times to break my addiction to sweets and grow my hunger for spiritual things. I'm learning that fasting from social media does something similar. Tony Reinke wrote, "Food fasting severs us from the love of sugar. Digital fasting severs us from the sugar of self-approval."[1] When we lay down our misplaced hunger, we grow hungrier for the right things. **When we lay down our need to be approved, there's a chance we'll find that we already are. We are approved and chosen.**

Chosen. Yes, that's the word. We've landed on it now. We desperately want to be chosen. But the irony breaks my heart. We open up the World Wide Web and ask everyone in the world to choose us when the One who made the world already did! Why can't that be enough? Sadly, we spend our lives trying to get everyone else to choose us too.

Dear fasting friend, know this: before you were made, you were chosen. That's why God chose to make you in the first place. Whether anyone invites you to hang out this weekend or not, you were chosen by the One who chose to make you. *Other people's "likes" pale in comparison to His love.* Their affirmation affirms nothing; His affirmation affirms everything! God said it clearly, and I believe it: "Now faith is the assurance of things hoped for, the conviction of things not

Before you were made, you were chosen.

seen. For by it the men of old gained approval" (Heb. 11:1–2 NASB). Our faith in Christ is all that's required to gain God's approval!

Every time God lays His eyes on us, He sees us through the lens of the cross and says, "I only see chosen; I only see redeemed; I only see grace, because I only see My Son." When God looks at you, He sees Jesus, because Jesus exchanged places with you on the cross: your sinful state for His perfect grace. Because you chose Jesus, you are always chosen. Your faith in the One who made you right makes you right today and tomorrow and the next day too. You can stop chasing it down now, online or anywhere else. You have nothing to prove, because you've been approved.

Am I now trying to win the approval of human beings, or of God? Or am I trying to please people? If I were still trying to please people, I would not be a servant of Christ. (Gal. 1:10)

What a relief to make a clean break of it. This forty-day break holds the power to break us from our unhealthy way of looking to people for what God has already given us. If you want to be wanted, focus on how much He wanted you, then purpose to want Him more. He chose you, so choose Him back. Let that be your focus. The God who spun the galaxies into place can still your spinning heart with the simple knowledge that He loves you and approves of you every day. The One who breathed the firmament into existence can breathe His breath into every old wound that causes you to wonder, *Am I enough?* God's answer is always a demonstrative, "Yes!"

If you agree with me but don't know how to let that reality fill your hungry-to-be-loved heart, invite the Lord to heal your wounds. You don't have to reach out online for the love you didn't receive in your formative years. Let the love of God fill you now. If you didn't feel chosen around the elementary school lunch table, accept the fact that you're chosen today. You don't have to post about every lunch date you go on. Allow the love of the Lord to heal your hurts and change the way you live your real life and your online life. You are worthy of love.

Worthy. Working hard to be found worthy hardly ever works. Whether online, in the cafeteria line at school, *You are worthy of love.* or in line for a promotion at work . . . all that effort is just another distraction from a simple life of devotion to the One who made us worthy. Worthy, chosen, approved, accepted, wanted, and loved.

Dear Lord, Holy Spirit, Help me to stop looking through the broken lens of old wounds to other people for their approval! Your love and approval are all I need—all I ever needed. In the name of the One who made the world and then chose to make me too, I am chosen! Amen.

One More Thought

When we don't feel chosen, special, or accepted, it sometimes creates a longing so large we behave in ways that are not in line with our beliefs, from what we wear to what we share.

If you struggle to believe down to your core that you are accepted, garnering the acceptance of others becomes your chief ambition. That unhealthy hunger holds the power to throw you off your equilibrium, causing you to become unstable and fall. **Temptation has the upper hand when you don't know whose hand holds you.** However, when you take God's hand and take Him at His word, believing that Christ already accepted you, your place in His palm is secure. The pull to post for the "likes" of the world loses its power, because the pull of His acceptance is enough. Each day and each post has less to do with you finding love and more to do with the fact that you already are loved.

DAY 18

El Roi

> She gave this name to the Lord who spoke to her: "You are the God who sees me," for she said, "I have now seen the One who sees me."

Genesis 16:13

Recently, a friend of mine posted this question online: Which of God's names resonates with you most deeply? The answer came to me quickly. The name I thought of didn't sound like one of today's trendy downtown churches: The Vine, Living Water, Morning Star, or The Way. Nor was it mentioned in the great prophecy of the Messiah's birth: "And he will be called Wonderful Counselor, Mighty God, Everlasting Father, Prince of Peace" (Isa. 9:6). Though every one of God's names inspires me to take a *Selah* pause as I dwell on some incredible facet of God's multifaceted goodness, in that moment I did not consider any other name but one: El Roi.

You may know the story of Abraham and Sarah and how God promised to build a nation for Himself through them. They were old when the promise came, and Sarah had been barren throughout their entire marriage. It was hard for her to believe at first—she laughed in disbelief at God's promise of a child—and it became even harder as the years passed and her womb remained empty. Finally, in a last-ditch effort to see God's word to them fulfilled, Sarah gave her Egyptian bondservant, Hagar, to Abraham as a concubine in hopes that Hagar would conceive and bear them a child.

Hagar did get pregnant, but almost immediately there was strife between the two women. We're told that Hagar despised Sarah, and that Sarah blamed Abraham for the mess. That's when Abraham gave Sarah permission to do with Hagar what she wished. Sarah then abused her slave until Hagar ran away.

Oh, the heartache of Hagar's plight. I can imagine Hagar, pregnant and alone, stopping beside that spring in the desert, just off the road to Shur. It was there the angel of the Lord appeared to her, speaking a blessing over her life and the life of her child and telling her to return to her mistress. After that encounter, Hagar gave God this new name: El Roi, the God who sees me.

> She gave this name to the LORD who spoke to her: "You are the God who sees me," for she said, "I have now seen the One who sees me." (Gen. 16:13)

From the time I was young I have had a strong sense that God was not only real but really close. I felt His love and sensed His eyes upon me. Like Hagar, I developed this awareness of His presence in a season when I felt very much alone. As a child I often struggled to experience my father's love after my parents' divorce. I had a deep fear that my dad would leave me as he had left our home. One evening, when I was about nine years old, I was waiting in front of our house for him to pick me up. Though he wasn't late, I was insecure. Life felt uncertain, as did my dad's presence. As I sat on the front porch,

The One who knit me knows me.

waiting and worried, the Lord's nearness suddenly overwhelmed me as it never had before. His Spirit, intimately and tenderly, came to my spirit. I knew He was there. I knew He saw me.

Over the years, God continued to reveal His presence in the broken places of my relationship with my dad. How kind of Him to use those struggles with my earthly father to flesh out the unseen but very real presence of my heavenly Father.

I remember going for a hike in the mountains with my dad and his new wife when I was in my early teens. The location was a familiar spot beside a mountain spring, one that our family had hiked for years. Dad wore a camera around his neck and stopped a time or two to snap photos of his wife, but never of me. Even now, thirty years later, I remember the pain of not feeling seen. However, beside that mountain spring, I had an encounter with God much like the one Hagar had beside her desert spring. God communicated to me so clearly: *I see you. And not only do I see you, I'm snapping pictures and treasuring every moment I spend with you.* Ever since that day, I have had this profound expectation that when I arrive at God's eternal home in glory, I will find my room decorated with the pictures my heavenly Father was taking of me all along.

Perhaps this is a childish, theologically inaccurate vision of heaven, but it brings me great comfort. The One who knit me knows me. **The One who saved me sees me. I am His and He is mine.** His name is El Roi, and His eyes have been on me all the time. In light of this vision, I don't need to be taking selfies and posting them every day. God is capturing every moment of my life. I don't need to fight to be seen; I am seen.

When we know the God who sees us, we can stop posting for a hot minute and find our rest in the fixed gaze of His unwavering love. His love doesn't trend; online algorithms don't change it either. He's always near, always present, always watching, always capturing memories with us. This is why we don't need the eyes of humankind to affirm or approve. It's the same message I gave you yesterday, I know, but I want to make sure you know how dear you are to the One who loves dearly. He's always looking your way.

Multiple times throughout the Old Testament, God describes His people as the apple of His eye. Some translations say "the pupil" of His eye. Either way, these passages tell us that we hold God's attention and affection. I love the imagery in Deuteronomy 32:10:

> He found him in a desert land,
>   and in the howling waste of the wilderness;
> he encircled him, he cared for him,
>   he kept him as the apple of his eye. (ESV)

The Message version brings such tenderness to the scene:

> He found him out in the wilderness,
> in an empty, windswept wasteland.
> He threw his arms around him, lavished attention on him,
> guarding him as the apple of his eye.

This is why we can pray Psalm 17:8 right back to Him: "Lord, keep me as the apple of Your eye." This is why we lift our gaze from our phones to our family, from our screens to the skies, from our distracting devices to the One to whom we are devoted.

In response to His generous seeing, let's stop worrying about whether we are seen and lift our eyes to see others whom He sees.

Here's today's final lesson: God is not just looking at *you*. His eyes are on all of us. Such knowledge is too wonderful; His vantage point too vast, immeasurable, and incredible. He sees us all. In response to His generous seeing, let's stop worrying about whether we are seen and lift our eyes to see others whom He sees. Our family and friends, first and foremost, but the lost and lonely as well. Perhaps, with your eyes open and your heart open too, you will come across a Hagar all alone, someone who needs to know she is seen by God. It's hard to be on the lookout for others when you're desperate to be noticed yourself.

God sees you; let that inspire you to see others today.

El Roi, Thank You for seeing me. May the fact that I am the "apple of Your eye" change my view of me and how I post and how I pray. I don't need to be seen by everyone at all times because I know You see me at all times. In the name of Jesus, the One who came to earth to literally lay His eyes upon humanity. Thank You and amen.

DAY 19

The Grass Isn't Always Greener

Keep your lives free from the love of money and be
content with what you have, because God has said,
"Never will I leave you;
never will I forsake you."

Hebrews 13:5

I was newly married when I learned to keep my first house on Brunchberry Lane in Plano, Texas. Our home was more than I ever dreamed of, and I was content. In the dining room I hung a wall of wedding pictures, then reupholstered chairs to complement the curtains. My husband and I painted the kitchen a bright yellow, and since the room was shaped like a barn, we accented one wall "barnyard red" and decorated the open shelves with roosters. Roosters were all the rage in Texas in the early 2000s. On the small patio beside our itty-bitty backyard pool, I filled a three-tiered shelf with a cascading collection of potted herbs.

Having grown up living in only one house my whole life, I imagined we would stay in this home forever. Though we didn't yet have children, I knew which room would one day become the nursery and which we would use as a guest room until another child came along.

In those days, back before HGTV and Pinterest showed us what we didn't have, we were a culture crazy for magazines. Most monthly periodicals are online now, but back then I'd keep my magazines stacked beside the couch, having turned down the corners of the pages showcasing my favorite kitchen countertops, the wainscoting I longed to put up in the family room, the decorative chandelier hanging over the pink crib in the nursery, the perennial gardens lining the front of each Cape Cod–style house.

My favorite was *Better Homes & Gardens*. Looking back now, I'm convicted by the name. Though I was happy with our home and smitten with the handsome husband I shared it with, I'd spend hours dreaming up ways to make it *better*. Don't get me wrong; I don't think there's anything wrong with making your home beautiful or planting a garden full of flowers and fruit trees. But we need to lift our eyes higher than that. Spending one's life always looking for *better* is never best. The best life is the content life.

Spending one's life always looking for better is never best. The best life is the content life.

Today we don't have to pick up a magazine to see what other people's carefully curated homes look like. Right there, in our palms and pockets, is a portal into homes that are better, lives that are more beautiful, gardens that are lusher, children who are more obedient and who smile for the camera and obviously adore their siblings. Today, people struggle with comparison more than ever before because everyone else's lovely lives are constantly on display.

While some people look with a critical eye on what others post, the more common response is to turn the criticism on ourselves. *My countertops are never that clean . . . the notes I scribble in my Bible never look so lovely . . . my friends' pictures are always so beautiful; what filter are they using? My husband doesn't snap pictures of me smiling with our children, he doesn't BBQ, he never takes me on a #datenight, let alone a weekend getaway. . . . How come everyone else's home looks like a spread in* Better Homes & Gardens *when I'm stuck here in a messy house?*

Can you relate? Do you feel the pressure to keep up with the virtual Joneses? I see and feel it too. What's more, it shapes the way I curate my own online display. I slide everything else off the countertop before taking a picture of the snack tray I'm delivering to my kids outside as they take turns cannonballing into the pool. That pile of clutter I swept away isn't the only thing I edited out of my post. The truth is that my kids haven't shared a contented afternoon together in eons, with or without snack trays. They've been bickering like crazy and driving me to tears.

These perfect posts are the highlights, but they don't allude to the hundred lowlights that separate each published picture. That's what most of us do on social media. We digitally scrapbook the moments that are best and quietly, privately, deal with the rest. Don't you see: the grass isn't greener; our neighbors are just selective about what they show us . . . and they use a filter to make it look even better. We're comparing our real lives to their carefully curated images. So, what's the application? Not looking? Not posting? While that can help in the short-term, it's not the long-term answer for most. Though we are taking a forty-day break from social media, we need a better answer. I suggest that Christ is that answer.

Christ is at the core of the Scriptures that focus on our contentment. The verse I shared at the beginning of today's reading is a perfect example. "Keep your lives free from the love of money and be content with what you have, because God has said, 'Never will I leave you; never will I forsake you'" (Heb. 13:5). When we focus on what we have—Christ's constant presence—instead of what we don't have, we are content. When He is at the center of our lives, He crowds out the desire for more.

When we have Christ, we have enough. However, when we lose touch with Christ as our "enough," we never have enough. He is the secret to our contentment: the secret to being content in our real lives and our on-line lives too. Because He is our portion, our

When we have Christ, we have enough.

"enough," with Him our days brim with beauty. Not the sort of beauty captured and shared online but the quiet contentment of His abiding nearness.

> Whom have I in heaven but you?
>   And earth has nothing I desire besides you.
> My flesh and my heart may fail,
>   but God is the strength of my heart
>   and my portion forever. . . .
> But as for me, it is good to be near God. (Ps. 73:25–26, 28)

Christ is our portion. With Him we're all filled up and satisfied. Therefore, Christ, at the center of our lives, is the centerpiece of our peace. Here's one more passage to help us believe it to be true:

> I've learned by now to be quite content whatever my circum-stances. I'm just as happy with little as with much, with much as with little. I've found the recipe for being happy whether full or hungry, hands full or hands empty. Whatever I have, wherever I am, I can make it through anything in the One who makes me who I am. (Phil. 4:11–13 MSG, emphasis added)

There is no better life than the life spent in intimate friendship with God. Enjoying His nearness and His promise to remain with us as we remain with Him is our best life. No better home, no better garden, no better post, no better family or family portrait, no better anything. When Christ is your best, you'll not strive for better!

Lord, You are the best. Life with You is the best life. I don't want to stumble around comparing myself to others, lacking contentment another day. Whether I'm renting a room in someone's back-alley apartment or living in that Cape Cod house surrounded by lush gardens, as long as I'm living with You, Lord, I'm happy with my home. Make Your home in me today. No filter needed in this beautiful, contented, comparison-free life with You!

In Jesus's name, Amen.

DAY 20

Red Lights

You are tempted in the same way that everyone else is tempted.

But God can be trusted not to let you be tempted too much, and he will show you how to escape from your temptations.

1 Corinthians 10:13 CEV

By the time this book is in your hands, my sons will be seventeen, fifteen, and thirteen. As I'm writing this my oldest, Caleb, is still fifteen. Not old enough to get his license, but he will be soon. Needless to say, publishing is a long, slow, and arduous process. Getting my sons prepared for life, however, takes even longer.

I wonder, am I preparing my soon-to-be-driver to be a focused driver? Or am I modeling how to be a distracted driver, as I fiddle with my phone at red lights? What am I teaching him? Caleb sees me open the Word and go to church and serve others, but what else does he see me do daily? Does he see the way I reach for my phone to change music or plug in directions as we drive around town? If I want him to put his phone away before he slides behind the wheel of a car and navigates thousands of pounds of steel down the highway, I've got to show him what that looks like.

When I'm on the road, whether alone or with my kids, and a ping notifies me of a message, I am tempted to pick it up, wondering, *Is my husband trying to tell me something? Did my dentist just confirm my appointment? Has a friend commented on the vulnerable post I left on Instagram before leaving the house? Has my Amazon order been delivered?* While not one of those messages is a matter of life or death, my choice to check or not check them could be—and not only in that moment but in other moments years from now, when my kids do what they saw me do. I don't want them to check their phones as they drive because they saw their mom and dad doing it. In short order, Caleb will have a steering wheel in his hands. Am I steering him right?

I'm convicted by this verse on generational sin: "So while these nations worshiped the LORD, they also served their idols; their children likewise and grandchildren, as their fathers did, so they do to this day" (2 Kings 17:41 ESV). Ouch.

This chapter may hurt a little, but we have to stop texting and driving! It's the law, after all. Perhaps you know that, but still the impulse to pick up your phone is stronger than your knowledge of right and wrong. That *compulsion* is what I want to focus on today. Whether or not you have children, whether or not you think you're safe, whether or not the Holy Spirit has convicted you about it . . . do you still keep on checking your messages like you don't have the power to say no?

What I hope to drive home today isn't safe-driving habits but the idea that God must be firmly seated behind the wheel of our lives. **Jesus Christ, through the indwelling presence of His Holy Spirit, must be the only driver seated securely in the driver's seat.** When we don't have the self-control to say no to our phones while we are behind the wheel, it's because something else has too much control over us. Anything or anyone other than Christ in you that rules your daily choices is a false master. God alone has the authority to lead us. When we obey Him, our lives testify to His authority. When we do not obey Him, however, and follow every impulse, we testify to someone else sitting in the driver's seat of our out-of-control lives.

This message isn't just about phones and driving. If you must have anything other than Christ to get you through the day—*I must have that food, I must have that drink, I must look at those images online, I must sleep with that person, I must sneak that vape, I must pick up my phone at each red light*—then you are driving straight into the twin headlights of addiction and idolatry. Your mind may tell you right from wrong, but if your impulses boss you around like a bully, you need help. And the help you need is the Helper.

> If you must have anything other than Christ to get you through the day ... then you are driving straight into the twin headlights of addiction and idolatry.

When Jesus ascended into heaven, He told His followers He would send them a Helper (John 15:26 NASB). The Holy Spirit is that Helper. If you have accepted God's gracious gift, then the Helper Himself is in you, ready to help! First John 4:4 tells us, "Greater is He who is in you than he who is in the world" (NASB).

You are not powerless. **The Holy Spirit of God in you is stronger than the impulse to pick up your phone hundreds of times each day.** Jesus promised, "I will ask the Father, and he will give you another advocate to help you and be with you forever—the Spirit of truth. The world cannot accept him, because it neither sees him nor knows him. But you know him, for he lives with you and will be in you" (John 14:16–17).

God-in-you is stronger than any impulse you face today. God is stronger than the tempter and the temptation. He is the way out of every temptation that feels like a compulsion. The Bible says, "You are tempted in the same way that everyone else is tempted. But God can be trusted not to let you be tempted too much, and he will show you how to escape from your temptations" (1 Cor. 10:13 CEV).

Jesus referred to Himself as "the way" (John 14:6). He is the Way to the Father, yes, but He is also the Way out of your addiction to your phone. He is stronger than the strong pull. Instead of running headlong into temptation, justifying why it is okay to check your digital device on the road, run to the only One who is the one-way road out of every temptation.

God-in-you is stronger than any impulse you face today.

Today when you come to a red light and reach for your phone, stop and ask yourself who is in the driver's seat of your life at that moment. What you display today will influence future generations. With Christ in you, you can live a life modeling obedience. Your phone is not the boss of you; Master Jesus is!

Lord, I don't want to be ruled by my compulsions, as though I have no say in what I do. I want to be ruled by You. You are strong, and Your strength in me is greater than any temptation I face. You are the strong Way out of temptation. I'm blazing a trail for future generations to know You as the Master of their days as well, so I am asking for Your help. May Your voice be the only notification my family needs to navigate through this life. Be our internal GPS, Holy Spirit, wherever we're headed today. Amen.

It's the Law

If you regularly pick up your phone when you're behind the wheel, commit to keeping your phone far away from you when you drive during these fasting days. And when your fast is over, keep putting it away when you're driving. This isn't a short break. This is an invitation to hit the brakes on that behavior. It's the law. Obey it for your safety and the safety of generations to come.

DAY 21

Famous

God didn't send me out to collect a following for myself, but to preach the Message of what he has done,
collecting a following for him. And he didn't send me
to do it with a lot of fancy rhetoric of my own, lest the
powerful action at the center—Christ on the Cross—be
trivialized into mere words.

1 Corinthians 1:17 MSG

One of my grandfathers was a preacher and the other was
an evangelist. Both took the stage in order to preach the
gospel fifty years ago. The one stood in front of a congregation on Sunday mornings, teaching the Word after the organ played.
The other put on riveting science shows at the annual World's Fair
from 1962 to 1974 and used that platform to point men, women,
and children to the God who created this natural world with all its
wonders. Today, you can google their names and find a little bit of
information about each man, but that's it—an old picture of a brick
church along with an obituary of the preacher, and a review of the
show, "Sermons from Science," for the evangelist.

They never made names for themselves. Neither of my grandpas collected large followings; they were simply in the business of collecting followers of Christ. They weren't looking for disciples of their own; they were looking to make disciples for the Master.

In this digital age, things are a bit more complicated for those who share their faith online. When we post online, we constantly get feedback about how many people "like" what we share. Every moment of every day, we know exactly how many people are following us as we follow Jesus. It's hard to not get caught up in a numbers game, as though this life is some sort of popularity contest.

I imagine it's hardest for teens today. If you are a young person reading this book, having shut down your social media apps for forty days, I'm proud of you! You're a rebel. **Keep pursuing a friendship with Christ first and foremost and trust Him to provide the other friends you need.** Really, that's a lesson for us all.

Whether your online focus is making friends, keeping in touch with friends, or sharing Christ with your friends, it's common to fixate on how many friends you have. The best thing to do is keep your eyes on the One you're following rather than on how many are "following" you.

Even if you consider social media your primary mission field, the ultimate goal is Christ followers, not Instagram followers. While it's true you have to have an audience to reach an audience, don't worry about that. Keep your eyes on Him, and He will use you to grow His kingdom. Kingdom growth is always more important than Instagram growth. Whenever I find myself doubling back to see how many people have tapped that little heart on one of my posts, I try to remember to check my own heart.

Kingdom growth is always more important than Instagram growth.

Here's a passage for us to pray anytime our motives are getting a little mixed up: "Search me, O God, and know my heart; try me and know my anxious thoughts; and see if there be any hurtful way in me, and lead me in the everlasting way" (Ps. 139:23–24 NASB).

Sometimes we start something with the desire to make much of God but end up making much of ourselves in the process. Though we want to promote God's name and fame, we get distracted with seeking our own fame. The desire to be popular is something we all need to guard against, which is why I pray regularly for God to search my heart.

I also pray Proverbs 30:8–9:

> [Lord,] give me neither poverty nor riches,
>   but give me only my daily bread.
> Otherwise, I may have too much and disown you
>   and say, "Who is the LORD?"
> Or I may become poor and steal,
>   and so dishonor the name of my God.

I plead, *Lord, don't give me too much, that I might forsake You. But also don't give me too little that I might curse You.* Not only do I ask this regarding how many "likes" I get on a post, I pray this concerning how many of my books sell, how much money I make, and how many radio shows and podcast interviews I'm asked to do. I even pray Proverbs 30:8–9 over my appearance. I'm getting older, and my face is doing weird things. (Don't you dare laugh at me!) For example, my forehead wrinkles funny over my right eye when I smile, and my eyebrows are getting droopier. Sometimes I think I look like Bert from *Sesame Street*. What's worse, everyone else online today is so beautiful and photogenic! I never thought of myself as vain until I started posting pictures for all the world to see.

That's why I ask the Lord to give me just the portion of this world's beauty that He wants me to have—no more, no less. Then

I remind myself that He is focused on my beautiful, devoted heart, not my aging face. Since I am committed to not obsessing about my looks, I try to put more effort into the hidden places of my spirit, where gravity has no power.

> Do not let your adorning be external—the braiding of hair and the putting on of gold jewelry, or the clothing you wear—but let your adorning be the hidden person of the heart with the imperishable beauty of a gentle and quiet spirit, which in God's sight is very precious. (1 Pet. 3:3–4 ESV)

When I find myself anxious about how I look or how many "likes" I get online, I remind myself whose fame I'm after and whose face I seek. If God's glory and praise are my chief delights, I won't be stressed when nobody likes what I have to say, and I won't be envious as younger, more beautiful women join the online conversation. This isn't about me. This world, though passing away, is preparing us for God's eternal kingdom. As I journey through this temporary world, I'm committed to keeping my eyes on Him, asking Him to help me bring as many people as I can to Him.

When my oldest child was about twelve years old, he announced that he was going to be either a rock star or a worship leader. I teased, "That's the same job, babe! It's just a matter of who gets the glory." While you could debate me on that, as there are plenty of secular artists who give all the glory to God and plenty of worship leaders who take the stage for themselves, the lesson is simply this: let's humble ourselves before the Lord, so that we might live to lift Him high, both now and forevermore.

When I find myself anxious about how I look or how many "likes" I get online, I remind myself whose fame I'm after and whose face I seek.

I know it's important for people who sell things online to grow their social media presence, but those of us promoting the gospel have to be very careful. Let it always be our utmost desire to see God's kingdom grow rather than our "platforms." **Let's live and post and promote His fame over our own.** Humble yourself and allow God to get all the glory!

Lord, Help me to keep my eyes on You! You are exceptional and deserve all the attention and all the praise and all our "hearts." ♥
In the most famous name of Jesus, Amen.

DAY 22

Are You Ready to Be God-Ready?

God sticks his head out of heaven.
   He looks around.
He's looking for someone not stupid—
   one man, even, God-expectant,
   just one God-ready woman.
He comes up empty. A string
   of zeros. Useless, unshepherded
Sheep, taking turns pretending
   to be Shepherd.
The ninety and nine
   follow their fellow.

Psalm 14:2–3 MSG

When God looks at you, what does He see? Has He found a God-ready woman or a God-expectant man? Has He caught you devoted or distracted—following hard after Him or hardly following Him at all?

123

When I traveled to Israel in the summer of 2018, I saw a shepherd walking along an ancient path in the hills of Bethlehem, a string of sheep in his wake. They walked behind their shepherd in a single-file line. I'd never seen anything like it before, and the image has stayed with me as a picture of how narrow the road is for those of us who are following Jesus.

It's nearly impossible for us to follow the Shepherd while following other sheep. Likewise, we can't stay in line behind Jesus when we're following everyone online. The online road is wide and distracting, and the virtual paths we wander down are endless. Even Jesus's most devoted sheep can lose their way if they take their eyes off Him. We're so distracted by everyone else! Even good and godly people—your family and friends, your pastor, your favorite worship leader or author—should never take the place of the Good Shepherd as your primary leader. It is His voice, above all others, you need to hear.

It's nearly impossible for us to follow the Shepherd while following other sheep.

Here is another sheep story Jesus told:

> Suppose one of you has a hundred sheep and loses one of them. Doesn't he leave the ninety-nine in the open country and go after the lost sheep until he finds it? And when he finds it, he joyfully puts it on his shoulders and goes home. Then he calls his friends and neighbors together and says, "Rejoice with me; I have found my lost sheep." I tell you that in the same way there will be more rejoicing in heaven over one sinner who repents than over ninety-nine righteous persons who do not need to repent. (Luke 15:4–7)

All these years later, and His followers are still like that one wayward sheep. Which is why "God sticks his head out of heaven . . . looking for someone not stupid," just "one man, even, God-expectant, just one God-ready woman" (Ps. 14:2 MSG). But our eyes can't see Jesus because they're on everyone else. Our ears can't hear Him either because they're listening to the worldwide chatter. Without meaning to, we've gone the way of the culture. Like the "ninety-nine," we're following after the ones online who are talking loudest and posting the prettiest pictures, and in turn we have become the "one" sheep who gets lost along the way. How wonderful that we have a Shepherd who never gives up on His rescue mission.

If you are a sheep who knows the Shepherd's voice but have fallen out of line as you've wandered online, perhaps God is using these fasting days to chase you down, throw you over His shoulders, and bring you back to His flock. It will require a measure of surrender on your part. A willful sheep who keeps running off eventually must be disciplined. Lovingly, for the benefit of the sheep, a good shepherd will even break the animal's leg so that it learns to stay close. I don't know about you, but I don't want that sort of discipline. I'd rather learn to be self-disciplined and stay close without the need for His intervention.

Wandering sheep can be devoured by jackals or find themselves lost for years. Back in 2004, a sheep named Shrek wandered off from his farm in South Island, New Zealand, and ended up living in a cave for six years before his owner found him again. During this time, his wool had grown thick and heavy. He carried the weight of his foolishness as a burden on his back. When he was finally sheared, sixty pounds of wool lay at his feet.[1] Can you imagine the relief that poor animal must have experienced as the weight fell from him?

If you are a sheep who's wandered off, you're likely carrying a heavy weight too: addiction and anxiety, loneliness and isolation, toxic relationships and unforgiveness, striving for success and fearing failure. **If these fasting days have brought you back to our shepherding Savior, or brought you to Him for the first time, allow Him to shear the heavy load from your back.** He longs to carry you and your burdens.

Following Jesus requires tremendous self-denial. No wandering off! Unfortunately, self-denial is in direct opposition to the message of our culture. We live in a generation that glorifies gluttony and instant gratification. We're told that we should be allowed to have and be and do whatever we want. All is relative, all is available, and all roads lead to the same green pastures. Except they don't. What the world says is not what the Word says. The Word says to be self-controlled, but the world says the bigger the better, more is more marvelous, and there is no need to wait.

If you want to follow Christ in this world, you must deny yourself a little of this world.

Today we carry with us, everywhere we go, a smorgasbord of apps to whet our appetite. The World Wide Web is a virtual feast, an opportunity for global gluttony. There is no reason to deny ourselves. Except Jesus, the Good Shepherd, said, "Whoever wants to be my disciple must deny themselves and take up their cross daily and follow me" (Luke 9:23). If you want to follow Christ in this world, you must deny yourself a little of this world. Again, every bit of this is countercultural. The rest of the sheep are back at the trough. Shoulders slumped forward, heads down. Scrolling through social media, watching movies, listening to music, overeating, overspending, and overdoing it all, all the time. But not you, not today. You're a sheep who is committed to following the Shepherd. Your head is lifted in an effort to be God-ready!

In the quiet of your fast, with both eyes and ears open, purpose to know the Shepherd's voice. In John 10:27 Jesus said, "My sheep listen to my voice; I know them, and they follow me."

Follow Jesus today. Deny yourself the right to live as the world lives, following everyone and consuming everything. Choose instead to follow the One who loves you so much that He'd chase you down anywhere in the world, shave the burdens off your shoulders, and carry you back to His fold.

God, You are constantly looking for the one who is looking for You, always intent on following You. I want to be that "one" who stays in line, even when I'm back online. It's going to take more than a little self-denial, more than a little countercultural living. You know this isn't going to be easy for me, and so, Holy Spirit, I'm asking for Your help. Help me to keep my eyes on You and my ears attentive to Your voice. In Your name, Shepherd Jesus, Amen.

A Message for Parents

A sheep without a shepherd is vulnerable online today. Young lambs are especially vulnerable. My husband and I are trying to protect our kids in this digital age by setting boundaries and teaching them self-control. Though it's countercultural, we don't allow them to have internet access on their phones until they are juniors in high school. In the meantime, we have firewalls on our family computers and tablets and don't allow computers in bedrooms or bathrooms. We're also training them how to not wander off online by spending time with them online. When our kids want to open up their first social media account, they are welcome to do it . . . on my phone. We don't want to be killjoys, overbearing, or unfair but to protect our little lambs from the wolves who prowl the World Wide Web. I won't be there to oversee my children's online habits much longer, so I'm teaching them to stay on the narrow path. I want my kids to be God-ready. I want them to follow Jesus rather than their culture. And I want to be God-ready too.

DAY 23

Keeping Your First Love First

If your right eye causes you to stumble, gouge it out and throw it away. It is better for you to lose one part of your body than for your whole body to be thrown into hell. And if your right hand causes you to stumble, cut it off and throw it away. It is better for you to lose one part of your body than for your whole body to go into hell.

Matthew 5:29-30

I find it poetic that the two body parts God focuses on in this passage about ongoing sin are the hand and the eye—the parts of the body that we use most directly with our digital devices. With our hands we hold them, with our eyes we behold them. What we cradle in our hands, we cradle in our hearts, yet God made our hearts to be His dwelling place.

When Jesus said the words above, it was in the context of adultery: "You have heard that it was said, 'You shall not commit adultery.' But I tell you that anyone who looks at a woman lustfully has already committed adultery with her in his heart" (Matt. 5:27–28).

When it comes to our relationship with social media and our online "friends," we can apply this passage in two ways. First, we must ask ourselves, *Is my love for social media adulterous? Do I love being social with them more than being social with Him?* I mentioned this earlier, but I'm bringing it up again now: although we want to want God most, many of us turn to social media more. We look at the world through our screens and lust after her beauty and her riches, her friendship and affirmation, rather than the beauty, riches, friendship, and affirmation of Christ. This type of adultery tempts most of us. **We scroll with our thumbs and consume with our eyes but are often too busy and too tired to invest in our love relationship with Him.** This may be why you committed to lay down your devices in the first place—in an effort to turn back to your first love.

Christ is known as the Bridegroom, and the church is called His bride. When we forsake that intimate relationship and pursue the world's love, we are as adulterous as the Israelites when they entered foreign lands, married unbelievers, and forsook God and His loving law. While our first-love devotion to Christ is the overarching, recurring invitation of this fast, there is also another warning for us here.

> *What we cradle in our hands, we cradle in our hearts, yet God made our hearts to be His dwelling place.*

Today we need to ask ourselves a second question: Are we using our digital devices to fan the flames of adulterous desire? Not surprisingly, social media is one of the leading contributors to both emotional and physical affairs.[1] Psychotherapist Joyce Marter wrote, "Social media seems to have added fuel to the fire of infidelity. . . . Former flames are just a click away. Appropriate relationship boundaries can become blurry. For example, when does casual messaging cross the line into an emotional affair?"[2]

Setting down social media for a season is good for us all, no doubt, but for those who are continuing relationships online with a former flame, today's challenge has the power to protect and even save your marriage (and theirs).

During our short engagement, Matt suggested we do something drastic: communicate with anyone we previously had a romantic relationship with and let them know we were getting married and wouldn't be available for a casual friendship with them in the future. Though there weren't a lot of people we had to reach out to, it was an uncomfortable thing to do. Facebook was brand-new, but I wasn't yet part of that network. I didn't yet have a cell phone either, just email, a landline, and a pager. I called all three of my ex-boyfriends and told them I was getting married and that I would no longer be in contact with them. The conversations were awkward and brief. In recent years two of the three have reached out to me with a friend request, but I simply ignored those invitations.

The other boundary Matt and I decided to implement was to get rid of all the gifts we had received from former flames. His were small and meaningful treasures kept in a shoebox. My gifts were larger and more practical: a desk, a stereo, a few pieces of art. It was a proactive measure to protect our imaginations from wondering and wandering. We cut off the friendships, we cast down the gifts, and we clung only to each other.

Today, I ask you to consider who you may need to "unfriend." Maybe a past boyfriend or girlfriend with whom you communicate via private messaging. Or maybe it isn't a former flame but the friendly dad who is always available to you when you cheer on your kids from the sidelines of their soccer games. Or perhaps it's that work colleague from a decade ago who used to invite you to grab a glass of wine when you went to conferences together. Nothing ever developed back then, but you still think of it. He may not be doing anything to tempt you now, and yet your thoughts are still . . . tempted. His posts cause you to linger and remember and lust.

Before you make your way back to the online social scene, honestly assess your online friends. If there is a specific person who tempts your eyes and emotions away from your spouse, make a plan. Even if you have not been inappropriate, casting down that one online friendship may be the most appropriate, thing you can do. If that is not enough, then perhaps you need to go so far as to "cast down" (or shut down) social media altogether.

And what about your relationship with social media in general? Maybe you're not tempted by a specific person as much as you are led astray by "all the people." Does the phone in the palm of your hand lead you away from the One who holds you in the palm of His expansive hand? Don't just set some private boundaries and confess your sin to the Lord but go the distance. Cut off any adulterous relationship, whether it's with a person or social media altogether. You know what you need to do to keep your first love first.

Does the phone in the palm of your hand lead you away from the One who holds you in the palm of His expansive hand?

The choices you make today may feel drastic, but they are small compared to the love relationship you're actively protecting—with your Bridegroom and, if you are married, with your spouse.

Dear Lord, I claim You as my first love. Continue to show me what adultery looks like online. Convict me of any sin I need to repent of and turn from. Convict me also of the temptations I've let remain, temptations that could ultimately lead me astray. Help me to cut off ties with anyone who tempts me away from You or my spouse. I'd rather cut off a casual friendship than cut my family and wound us all. With Your Spirit's faithful help, I commit these things to You and will obey. In the name of Jesus, my eternal Bridegroom. Amen.

DAY 24

Enough Is Enough!

For, as I have often told you before and now tell you again even with tears, many live as enemies of the cross of Christ. Their destiny is destruction, their god is their stomach, and their glory is in their shame. Their mind is set on earthly things.

Philippians 3:18–19

Social media was a good place for us to start our fast, but it's just the tip of the iceberg when it comes to what we consume, online and offline. There's so much more we gobble up. Whether ingesting a string of silly memes, binge-watching endless episodes of HGTV, drooling over Pinterest while looking for decadent desserts, or buying every snarky T-shirt advertised in a sponsored post . . . we're all left with protruding bellies full of nothing at all and everything at once. **Our problem isn't social media. It's not even the internet. Our problem is our perpetual appetite for more.**

The apostle Paul said, "For, as I have often told you before and now tell you again even with tears, many live as enemies of the cross of Christ. Their destiny is destruction, their god is their stomach, and their glory is in their shame. Their mind is set on earthly things" (Phil. 3:18–19). While I don't think of myself as actively living in opposition to the gospel, I identify with the idea that my stomach is my god. Though I don't want it to be true, my metaphorical stomach is often more my god than God is. When it growls for more of this or more of that, I lack the self-control and God-control necessary to say no. No to my phone, no to another purchase, no to a leftover brownie. Social media isn't the only thing I turn to in an effort to fill the holes in me. I consume and consume and consume . . . and I know I'm not alone.

We've spent the first half of this fast lifting our eyes from our online consumption in an effort to consume more of God and savor the living, breathing blessings in our midst. However, I wonder, as you have lifted your eyes to life beyond your phone, have you found you are consuming other things with the same insatiable hunger? The food you eat, the purchases you make, the movies you watch?

When you stop at Chick-fil-A for another cup of sweet tea followed by a trip to Target, you may have a few moments of pleasure and fun, but it doesn't last. Consumerism, despite its promise to bring personal satisfaction, never does. More clothes and books can't meet your deepest needs either. All the throw pillows that fill a bed can't fill your heart when your stomach is your god. No matter how much stuff you cram in your house, how much entertainment you feed your eyes, or how much you drink, your belly still growls, *I want, I want, I want . . .*

A wanting life never leads to a satisfied life.

This fast is not about your screen habits as much as it is about your habitual hunger.

Perhaps your consumerism has less to do with an empty shelf and more to do with an empty self.

Perhaps your consumerism has less to do with an empty shelf and more to do with an empty self. Today, I encourage you to prayerfully consider what else you're turning to regularly instead of turning to Him. **Every fast should be an "anything fast" as God reveals the things that hold you back from the full life available to you in Christ.**

Perhaps you don't need a social media fast as much as you need a fast from shopping. I'm not talking about not buying essentials. Children's shoes need replacing, groceries need replenishing, toilet paper runs out. But if you spend your life spending, *you* will eventually be spent. Always consuming but never satisfied. Consider, therefore, laying down your perpetual purchases (whether online or in line at your favorite store) for the next sixteen days and invite God to speak to your heart (and your stomach) about how your shopping habits might need to change even after this fast is through.

Here are a few simple boundaries that may help.

Budget. Many people find that a budget helps them to hem in their spending. A budget has worked for me, even in seasons when I could justify spending more because there was a bit more.

I also find I shop less when I go to the store less. I don't want my stomach to be my god, and if I go to the store each time I feel the impulse, then God isn't controlling my life . . . my insatiable appetite is. That's why I keep an old-fashioned shopping list in my kitchen (though sometimes I add to it as a note on my phone when I'm out and about).

Eggs
Laundry detergent
Ziploc baggies
Cough drops
Legal-sized notepad . . .

Schedule. Another thing that has helped me practice self-control is shopping on a schedule. A disciplined routine keeps us from spending and living in an undisciplined way. With the help of a budget, a shopping list, and a schedule, you'll be less likely to give in to every impulse. If an impulse does seize you, seize it right back. Hold it captive and wait a bit. Don't let it have mastery over you. You already have a Master.

When Target is your target, you'll miss the bull's-eye entirely. You've got to aim higher. If you need a 40-Day Shopping Fast, go for it! The same One who convicted you to set down your phone can help you set down your credit card too.

A disciplined routine keeps us from spending and living in an undisciplined way.

Lord, Enough is enough! I'm ready to live as though You are enough. Each time I have a hankering for more, I want to actively choose "No more." You are my God, not my stomach. I'm choosing to live like that's true! In the satisfying name of Jesus, Amen.

DAY 25

Savor the Savior

As a deer pants for flowing streams,
so pants my soul for you, O God.
My soul thirsts for God,
for the living God.

Psalm 42:1-2 ESV

When I was a child, my parents took me to church on Tuesday nights for youth group. We played games, sang songs, and listened to a Bible lesson. A few times a year the church would invite families to come early for a church-wide spaghetti dinner. Pots of pasta with meat sauce, platters of garlic bread, bowls of salad, pitchers of lemonade, and pans of brownies filled one long table. It's the only food I remember being served at church, except for the grape juice and crackers at the communion table.

I believe that it's biblical to break bread together. Jesus ate with His disciples, reclining at the table with those He loved. He joined sinners around the table too. When people came to hear

Him speak and found themselves miles from town and out of food, He fed them. He also cooked. One of the first things Christ did for His disciples after His resurrection was make them breakfast.

Feeding one another is surely an act of love. One of the ways my mom has always shown love for her kids and grandkids is by cooking for us. Nobody makes better baked chicken and sweet potatoes than my mom. Nowadays I communicate love the same way to my family. It is my hope that you'll use some of the time you've gained from stepping away from social media to get around the table with those you love.

But over the years, I've come to find that I don't only cook to show love to my family and friends. I also bake to alleviate my stress and anxiety. When I'm overwhelmed with family stress or work deadlines, I run to food to find relief. I crave cheesecake and sugary beverages. Is that something you struggle with too?

Today, I want to invite you to consider if you need to lay down your eating habits on the altar of this fast. Are you overeating or emotionally eating—eating to self-medicate your pain, mask your loneliness, or fill some other void? While we love to eat, we don't want to live to eat. Even a whole foods diet can distract us from the holy work God wants to do in our lives. **When food is our focus, we miss a life focused on Christ.** That's why I regularly return to this prayer:

> Search me, God, and know my heart;
>   test me and know my anxious thoughts.
> See if there is any offensive way in me,
>   and lead me in the way everlasting. (Ps. 139:23–24)

During our annual sugar fast, I regularly ask people, "What else are you running to in lieu of Jesus?" The number one response I hear from my fasting friends is "social media." Now, during this fast from social media, I'm inviting you to consider whether you turn to food in your sadness, your loneliness, or your boredom. Is it possible that your eating habits mirror your online habits? All day long, checking in and nibbling. All day long, mindlessly eating, mindlessly scrolling. Do you hide in the pantry with a bag of granola, scrolling through Instagram? Do you mindlessly lose yourself in a bottomless bowl of chips and salsa as you watch show after show at night? Are you distracted with a phone in one hand and a fork in the other?

Comfort food is a sad substitute for the Great Comforter.

If so, know this: food isn't the answer. Remember, Christ said, "Come to Me when you are weary and heavy laden" (see Matt. 11:28). Comfort food is a sad substitute for the Great Comforter. And yet, the tendency for many of us is to run to food instead of running to Him.

In *A Hunger for God*, John Piper wrote:

> If you don't feel strong desires for the manifestation of the glory of God, it is not because you have drunk deeply and are satisfied. It is because you have nibbled so long at the table of the world. Your soul is stuffed with small things, and there is no room for the great. God did not create you for this. There is an appetite for God. And it can be awakened. I invite you to turn from the dulling effects of food and the dangers of idolatry, and to say with some simple fast: "This much, O God, I want you."[1]

The purpose of this fast is not to simply step away from distractions but to exchange those distractions for real-life devotion. To whet your appetite for God so that you turn to Him—not online distractions, food, alcohol, or anything else—to satisfy your hunger.

All of us, to varying degrees, struggle with soul sadness. Which is why we all need to learn coping skills when the sad waters rise. Self-medicating the pain with a glass of wine, nicotine, or a quick detour past the Starbucks drive-thru window will never help us long term. We might experience momentary relief, but it doesn't last. **Each** time we turn back to the same false filler, it becomes more like a false god. It was never sugar's job to make us happy, never social media's job to fill our lives with deeply satisfying relationships, and never alcohol or caffeine's job to get us through our hardest days.

Have you been self-medicating your pain, loneliness, or boredom by overeating? Long before you opened your first Facebook account, was your face in the pantry, looking for the answer to every sad question? Would setting down your food addiction during these remaining days help you to break free from another stronghold that is holding you back from experiencing God's strong hold? Might fasting from snacking increase your hunger and thirst for Him? When you finally set down the things you use to self-medicate, you'll find the Great Physician true to His name.

I started this chapter by sharing my memory of our spaghetti dinners at church. They were sweet times of fellowship indeed. However, the Holy Spirit knows what we need most of all: less food fuel, more holy fuel. Missionary and evangelist Reinhold Bonnke once wrote, "The less Holy Spirit we have, the more cake and coffee we need to keep the church going."[2] As we fast, let's remember that the goal of fasting is always feasting—on Christ. Whatever distractions you have given up, the focus must be on what you're gaining: devotion to Him. If food is a distraction hindering your devotion, fast from food in some way as well these next fifteen days.

> *When you finally set down the things you use to self-medicate, you'll find the Great Physician true to His name.*

Lord, I don't want to self-medicate with food or my phone. I want You, Great Physician. Help me to enjoy the gift of breaking bread with my loved ones, but help me to turn most regularly to You, the Bread of Life. In Jesus's satisfying name, Amen.

DAY 26

Liquid Courage

Some trust in chariots and some in horses,
but we trust in the name of the Lᴏʀᴅ our God.

Psalm 20:7 ESV

When I was a child, my mom would wake up early and start her coffee maker, then press play on the CD player. The rich aroma of beans brewing would intermingle with the gentle strains of George Winston's piano solos as they wafted down the hall and into my little-girl room. After making breakfast and packing lunches, Mom would come into my room singing, "Rise and shine and give God the glory glory . . ." with the scent of coffee and sweet cream on her breath.

Now that I have children of my own, I play George Winston's music as they wake up. I make my husband a cup of coffee when he's nearing the end of his shower and sing the same "Rise and Shine" chorus as I scramble eggs for the kids. Forty years later, both CD players and my mother's drip coffee maker are practically obsolete. Today I stream music from a wireless speaker in our kitchen simply by saying, "Alexa, play music by George Winston" as I pop a pod in our Keurig coffee maker. Some things have changed, but our morning routine and the world's love for coffee have not.

Only in recent years have I developed a taste for coffee. Last year, during my annual 40-Day Sugar Fast, I felt led to lay down my morning cup of joe beside my sweet treats. I didn't think much of it. Honestly, it didn't seem like a major sacrifice. However, I was shocked to discover how quickly my body had grown accustomed to the energy that single serving of caffeine provided me each morning. The first seven days hit me hard! More than feeling miserable physically, as I detoxed from my dependency, I

Is there anything else you need to unplug from in order to plug in to Christ?

felt miserable emotionally. I was sad—convicted that I had grown dependent on something other than Christ's strength to get me up and going each morning.

Perhaps you turn to coffee as your main source of strength, or maybe you trust some other drink to get you through your long days. Dr Pepper in lieu of the Great Physician; sweet tea in place of God's sweet, abiding presence; an afternoon cocktail followed by a nightly glass of wine when the stress gets to be too much. **Though Christ invited us, "Come to Me when you are weary," many of us still turn to a strong cup of coffee in our weariness as our main source of strength.**

This part of our fast has less to do with social media and everything to do with everything else. Is there anything else you need to unplug from in order to plug in to Christ? Perhaps your coffee machine is your charging station. You jokingly refer to your old-fashioned "drip" as your intravenous drip, keeping you alive some days. I know I might be stepping on toes, but it's good for us to do this. If we rely on caffeine or some other beverage, trusting that it can give us what we need to get our day going, we need a better battle plan. Psalm 46:1–3 promises us that God is our refuge and our strength, an always-present help when we're in trouble. As our refuge, He invites us to hide ourselves in Him, not behind our screens and certainly not in a bottle. We're invited to turn to Him as our strength-source morning, noon, and night for the ongoing courage we need to persevere in our daily challenges.

Just as hiding in the bathroom on Facebook hasn't helped you deal with stress, masking your exhaustion with your drink of choice won't give you the help you need either. The devil loves it when you think the answer to your weariness can be found at Starbucks rather than in the One who hung the stars. Satan adores it when you pour yourself a drink on the rocks rather than pouring your heartfelt prayers out to the One who said, "If they keep quiet, the stones will cry out" (Luke 19:40). Are you crying out to Him, as the daily battles wage around you, or do you cry out the car window to the barista as you order another latte on the go?

You need more than liquid courage, more than the strength and stamina caffeine provides. Each day is a battle that requires a better battle plan. Getting ready requires more than *getting caffeinated*. It's time to fully rely on the strength of the Lord our God each morning. Psalm 33:17 tells us, "Don't count on your warhorse to give you victory—for all its strength, it cannot save you" (NLT).

Even when caffeine provides energy and alcohol mimics courage, they can't give us what we truly need. We need a strong faith, not a strong cup of coffee. We need to stop looking to beans or brew to make us brave. This lesson isn't about coffee or alcohol, just like this fast isn't really about social media. This is entirely about what we place our trust in to get us through our days. I'm reminded of a funny meme that's made its way around the internet a few times, often on Monday mornings: "I need coffee to get up, but I need to get up to get my coffee."

We need a strong faith, not a strong cup of coffee.

While a cup of coffee may help you "rise," it cannot help you "shine" or "give God the glory glory." **We need God's strength to get up and go, to win our daily battles and live our days shining for Him.** In 1 Chronicles 5:20, God's people faced a literal foe. Instead of crying for another cup of coffee to give them the strength and courage they needed, "They cried out to him during the battle. He answered their prayers because they trusted in him."

Let's not place our trust in coffee, soda, energy drinks, alcohol, or anything else to give us strength for the days ahead. Perhaps, for the remainder of these fasting days, you may choose to unplug your coffee machine and plug in to Christ as your primary source of strength. With His help, when the sun rises you can rise too, singing, "Rise and shine and give God the glory glory."

Lord, You are my strength and my shield, a very present help in times of trouble (Ps. 46:1–3). I am choosing to depend on the power You provide to get me through my daily battles rather than a cup of coffee in the morning, an energy drink at noon, and a glass of wine at night. Thank You for making this less about social media and more about You—finding all I need in You. In the strong name of Jesus, Amen.

DAY 27

This Is Not a Game

You blind guides! You strain out a gnat but swallow a
camel.

Woe to you, teachers of the law and Pharisees, you
hypocrites! You clean the outside of the cup and dish,
but inside they are full of greed and self-indulgence.
Blind Pharisee! First clean the inside of the cup and dish,
and then the outside also will be clean.

Matthew 23:24–26

I was in the middle of a 40-Day Sugar Fast when I played my
first online game. I had made it nearly a decade with a smartphone before I caved. Though my children had downloaded
a couple of their favorite games and stored them on my phone
for long car trips, I had never felt the least desire to play one
myself—until I did.

It was a simple game of stacking vertical blocks that enticed me
that day. A toddler's game, really. Had they been actual wooden
blocks, my boys would have played with them years ago, building
on the rug in our family room as I made dinner. Now here I was,

a grown woman, leaning against the kitchen counter, distracted from the task of thawing frozen chicken breasts. Three days later, I was on level 37, still playing that ridiculous game.

That was the day I happened upon the above passage from Matthew 23. Verse 24 was a particularly hard pill to swallow: "You blind guides! You strain out a gnat but swallow a camel." I had strained out a sugar gnat only to gulp down a digital camel. For three straight days, I had missed the whole empty-bellied reason for my fast. I had given up the temporary pleasure of sugary sweets so that I might enjoy the satisfying sweetness of my Savior, only to let something else distract me.

Convicted, I deleted the game from my phone. However, it took me days to stop seeing the outline of blocks falling down into place everywhere I looked. Have you ever stared at a palm tree against a bright blue sky and then closed your eyes and found you were still able to see that silhouette? That's how it was with those silly falling blocks. I saw them everywhere. I saw them in the road as I drove, in the faces of my children, in the tiles at the grocery store—and when I closed my eyes to sleep at night, I saw them still. My eyes had grown accustomed to what they had been fixed upon. My ears had also memorized the happy little tune that accompanied the game. My eyes and ears and imagination all continued to be distracted, long after I stopped playing. For days, I was seeing my real life through the lens of that goofy game.

My eyes had grown accustomed to what they had been fixed upon.

While that was a bizarre experience, the reality is we're always looking at life through one lens or another—and what we focus on most becomes our worldview. It shapes what we see and how we see it—who we are and how we live. Through that lens, we interpret everyone and everything around us. When our lives are spent playing silly games, it's hard to be serious about our work. When we make entertainment our goal, we forget the things that should be goals. If you have a child or a spouse who is a gamer, you've likely heard them exclaim, "Oh, I forgot . . ." Whatever they were supposed to do, they forgot to do.

However, when our eyes are fixed on Christ, we remember what's most important: love God, love others. In this section of our fast, we're continuing to look up in order to discover the things beyond social media that have distracted us from our devotion to God and others. What have your eyes been fixed upon? What we have seen shapes what we will see.

If you've spent years being treated poorly and fixed your eyes on nurturing a bitter root in your heart, you may tend to see a bitter world and respond bitterly to those around you. If, as you were growing up, your eyes took in faces contorted with anger and your ears heard a sad string of putdowns and verbal abuse, you likely encounter those you meet with your guard up, prepared for a fight.

Video games can't fix all that, but Christ can when you fix your eyes on Him. **When our eyes are fixed upon the extravagant love of Christ, we look out into the world and see opportunities to love as He loves.** Looking at Christ prepares us to live like Christ.

Looking at Christ prepares us to live like Christ.

Oh, to be shaped by Christ! To keep our eyes on Him and see as He sees! To see ourselves as He sees us, and to see the world as He sees His world: ripe with opportunities to love and serve. Fasting from online visual stimulation should stimulate the eyes of our hearts. This sort of fast gives us fresh eyes to see not only our Savior but also those whom our Savior sees. I've said it before and I'll say it again: it's nearly impossible to see others with our noses in our phones. This is your one and only real life. *It's not a game!*

If you truly want to "level up," look up! Shut down your games. That's not to say life won't be fun. No. The Father's work is fun.

Not a mindless, online sort of fun, but a real-life adventure of living as Christ, seeing as Christ, loving as Christ. The word *Christian* literally translates to "little Christ." You, Christian, bear the image of Christ. Live like it.

Let's not play some Christian game, my friend. Let's not be hypocrites, calling ourselves Christ followers only to hide away behind some screen, unseen and unseeing. Playing the part in public but spending hours gaming in private. What is your one precious life about? If you've witnessed Christ, it's time you become His witness out in the world. Christ displayed in you—living and moving and having His way (Acts 17:28). That's a life without hypocrisy.

And let's not be Pharisees, either, with all the Christ-knowledge but none of Christ's love.

The Pharisees played a different sort of game—a loveless, self-absorbed game. They didn't see anyone but themselves. Their lens was clouded, their eyes distracted. They were so focused on the law they missed the One who fulfilled the law with His love. Theirs is a game we do not want to play. I'm not talking about Candy Crush now but rather the crushing game of looking the part without playing the part. What's the part? Following Christ.

God is inviting us to lift our heads and our eyes to His example: *Love Me, love others.* We must not profess to follow Christ while refusing to actually follow Him. Truly follow Christ, and your life will proclaim it! Fix your eyes on Him long enough, and He'll become the pattern you see everywhere you look.

Look up and keep looking up. The longer you gaze at Him, the more He will imprint Himself upon the eyes of your heart. If you have put down your games, now's the time to pick up the real life He has for you. As He becomes your view, may He become your life view. As you witness Him, may you become a witness for Him.

Dear Lord, I don't want to strain out the gnat of social media only to gulp down the camel of online games or anything else.

You have my full attention now. My eyes are on You. You're the lens through which I want to see. May witnessing Your life shape my life and make me Your witness. Holy Spirit, help me set down these digital distractions so that I might grow in devotion to You and those You are devoted to. In Jesus's name, Amen.

Married to a Gamer?

A few years ago, Matt and I signed up to be a mentor couple in a Sunday school class for newlyweds at our church. From the very first class, one thing was clear: many young couples were struggling in ways we never did. Primarily, many of the husbands were spending hours each day playing video games with friends online. They seemed to have more ambition to level up in their games than to level up in their career, and to win virtual prizes rather than the attention and affection of their spouse.

If you're married to a gamer and it causes stress in your marriage, use these fasting days to ask God to speak into and transform this area of your spouse's life. Commit to holding your thoughts and your words captive for the rest of these forty days, as you take your concerns to the Lord. Perhaps then, when your fast is over and you're ready to share what you've learned and what choices you hope to make going forward, you can invite your spouse to consider the effects of gaming on your family life. Invite him to set down his games for forty days and see for himself how looking up might allow him to level up at home. A gaming fast may be just what you both need to grow in intimacy together and with the Lord.

DAY 28

Streaming Distractions

Do not worship any other god, for the LORD, whose name
is Jealous, is a jealous God.

Exodus 34:14

After I graduated from college, I moved into a little apartment in North Hollywood, ready to pursue my career as an actress. Life was a busy blur of waiting tables and auditions. When I think back to that season in my life, I can hear the soundtrack of those days: Faith Hill, Steven Curtis Chapman, Indigo Girls, Etta James, Amy Grant. . . . Music was my roommate, and she was chatty. The alarm clock on my bedside table would go off with a song, and the music would roll on and on until I left the house and got into my car. When I turned the key in the ignition and the car revved to life, the radio static would buzz for a moment and then a new song would fill my car and attempt to fill me too. Always there was music.

Not that there is anything wrong with the music I was listening to. In fact, my radio dial was often set to a Christian station. The trouble was, I wasn't nearly as devoted to hearing from Christ. When worship songs stop you from hearing the One you're worshiping, there's a problem. I had a problem.

When worship songs stop you from hearing the One you're worshiping, there's a problem.

With all of that singing, I was missing the One who was singing over me. Zephaniah 3:17 tells us, "The LORD your God is with you, the Mighty Warrior who saves. He will take great delight in you; in his love he will no longer rebuke you, but will rejoice over you with singing." His was the love song I'd stopped hearing as I ran to my radio. That's why I fasted from music. I'd grown dependent on the noise that was canceling out the God song I most desperately needed to hear. So I said no to music in my car and no to music during meals, so that I could hear from the Lord in the quiet.

Today, we're connected everywhere we go, which makes connecting with our Savior harder than ever. We're wired for surround sound, and that makes it hard to hear the sound of our Savior's simple song. Every moment is filled with voices, and they tend to cover up the sweet, serenading Voice that matters most. Even praise songs can cancel out the silence necessary for an intimate time of private praise. Worship music is wonderful—unless we never get quiet enough to worship Him in our hearts. I'm not suggesting you need to fast from worship music, but I'm not saying you don't either. I am merely reminding you that our God is a jealous God (Exod. 34:14). He's jealous for our time and attention. He wants our eyes on Him and our ears open and listening for His voice. He's desperate for us to be desperate for Him. Before all else and above all else, He wants us to love Him most (20:3).

I loved Him a lot back then. I love Him even more now.

However, there are more distractions than ever these days, competing for our devotion. Back then, no one had ever heard of streaming. There were no podcasts, no apps for watching movies or TV shows. No digital downloads. My only phone was plugged into the wall. I had a television with thirteen channels and a rabbit-ear antenna. I didn't have cable, only a VHS player and a membership at Blockbuster Video.

Things are so different now. Just this morning I heard my husband ask our children to organize our DVDs and make up a bag or two to give away. I braced myself for a fight, knowing how much our boys love their movies, but they got to work without a struggle. I was surprised at first, then realized that my kids know they'll be able to find all of their favorite films streaming online.

Kids today watch a lot of TV. I thought my generation did, but back then we had to wait until Thursday night to catch the latest episode of our favorite show. If we missed it, we missed it. If we had to go to the bathroom, we held it until a commercial break. I can still hear my brother shouting, "Hurry up! It's coming back on." My idea of binge-watching television was running home from school each afternoon to watch reruns of *Little House on the Prairie*. Kids today can wear wireless earbuds under hoodies; we wouldn't even know if they're ceaselessly streaming music and podcasts.

This isn't about the younger generation. The problem for all of us is that if we are filling our eyes and ears with a steady stream of entertainment—whether music, television shows, movies, or podcasts—we are engaging in just another form of consumerism. We are looking to streaming distractions to fill us rather than the only One who truly can.

What is holding you back from the full life available to you in Christ? What else besides your phone do you need to lay down? Is it music? Podcasts? TV shows? Movies? TED Talks? If reality shows distract you from the reality of your own life, if sports commentators speak into the play-by-play moments of your day more than God does, if fictional love stories distract you from your own love story with the very real characters in your life . . . press pause.

Press pause on your favorite form of entertainment. Take out your earbuds and shut down Spotify, along with Netflix and Amazon Prime. Take a break from these distractions and give God your undivided attention, your eyes and ears and imagination. He's jealous for you and zealous for you. While His zeal is about communicating His love for you, His jealousy has everything to do with wanting your love in return.

When you press pause on these entertaining distractions, you hit play on the one very real life you've been given.

When you press pause on these entertaining distractions, you hit play on the one very real life you've been given. Remember, this isn't just a social media fast anymore; this fast is about laying down anything getting in the way of hearing His love song and singing it back to Him!

Dear Lord, Thank You for delighting in me; I want to delight in You too. Thank You for singing over me. I want to hear Your love song more than any other song streaming into my home and my heart. I want Your love story to be the only story I keep coming back to, day after day, night after night. If I'm going to binge-watch anything, let it be Your face, Your Word, Your story unfolding in my life. I don't want to miss out on my real life with You because I'm watching fictional characters living fictional lives. I don't want to miss out on the reality of You because reality shows fill my days. You are the Living Water, the only thing streaming that will ever make me full. In Jesus's name, Amen.

DAY 29

Extra! Extra! Read All about It!

I have told you these things, so that in me you may have peace. In this world you will have trouble. But take heart! I have overcome the world.

John 16:33

On April 29, 1992, I was nearing the end of my senior year of high school. I was attending a charter school near downtown Los Angeles and had an hour-long commute each day. On that particular afternoon, all of the students were given the news that rioting had broken out throughout the county. There was little reason given, only the instruction to remain on campus. No one was to leave the building.

A group of us made our way to an adjacent hallway where a TV was hung. One student dragged a chair into the hall from a nearby classroom. We quietly waited as he climbed up and turned on the TV. Immediately, images of chaos filled the screen. Young men carried televisions through shattered storefront windows and women yelled at officers who were attempting to bring order to mayhem. I remember hearing the newscasters' words: "The riots began in response to this afternoon's acquittal of the three policemen who had been charged with police brutality. . . . Just over a year ago they had nearly beaten to death construction worker Rodney King. . . . LAPD chief of police Daryl Gates is asking all residents to remain at home. . . . The National Guard are setting up headquarters at the Beverly Center in Beverly Hills. . . ."

My mom's office was only a few blocks from the Beverly Center mall, so I ran down the hall to a pay phone, fumbling for change. My call went straight to her voice mail. I tried home next and got our answering machine three times in a row. Unsure of what to do next, I wandered back to the room where my class was waiting for further instructions.

The fear was palpable. A few girls were crying, many of the boys were angry, and emotional debates arose as news of the acquittal spread. In the corner of the room a small group of students sat quietly in a circle, holding hands, heads bowed. When I approached their prayer meeting, they made room for me. We prayed for the city. We prayed for peace. We prayed for race relations to be healed and wrongs to be righted. Above all, we acknowledged Jesus as Lord and asked Him to bring peace to the world's chaos. It was a simple time of prayer. Then we sang "Great Is Thy Faithfulness" and "It Is Well with My Soul."

After we hugged, I picked up my backpack and walked out of the building to my car in the parking lot. It wasn't the smartest thing I ever did, but I did it. I left the school and took the freeway every news reporter had said to avoid. As I inched my way home, fires rising from buildings on both sides of the highway, I continued to pray for my city and my mom.

The house was empty when I arrived, so I turned on the TV to get the latest news. The phone rang. It was my friend April.

She and I were part of a local student coalition that peacefully protested against racial injustice. Together we had marched for Mandela's freedom, made signs, and written letters to politicians. We considered ourselves hippies on peaceful days, crusaders during times of injustice. As a seventeen-year-old woman of color, April was angry at the judge and the jury, and she was angry at men and women of color who were expressing their anger with violence. She was simply and overwhelmingly angry. When I suggested we pray together, she spat, "I'm too angry to pray!" and hung up the phone.

That's when my mom walked in with an armful of groceries. She had stopped at a store that was open and functioning peaceably and grabbed what she thought we might need for the next few days.

My memories of that day have stayed vivid for nearly thirty years. The images on the TV, the news updates, the prayers lifted in the corner of my high school classroom, the fires, and April's call. But over all of it, I remember a peace in my heart that transcended the chaos in my city. God was on His throne. He remained sovereign and good. I was encouraged then (and remain comforted as we continue to face racial inequality and unrest today) that this Bible promise is true: "In this world you will have trouble. But take heart! I have overcome the world" (John 16:33).

> Our understanding of the goodness and love of God must be the foundation upon which we stand.

I'm not suggesting we don't need to be concerned about the chaos we see around us. I'm not suggesting we don't petition and push back against evil. However, our understanding of the goodness and love of God must be the foundation upon which we stand, with our phones in hand and a stream of news pinging us around the clock.

How can a good God allow such evil? How can a merciful God allow such suffering? Those are good questions. And they are commonly asked by Christians and nonbelievers alike when pandemics shut down entire countries, tsunamis take out whole villages, and murderers go free. Where is God when a bill is passed allowing full-term abortions? Where is God when sex exploitation is at an all-time high? With upward of fifty *thousand* young women being trafficked just throughout the United States each year, where is God?[1]

Here's what we know to be true, based on the gospel: **God loves the world and every person in it. His love is expansive, and His emotions are tender.** He came to overcome the darkness with His love-light, and, whether it looks like it or not, He was successful! When God sent His Son into the mess of humanity to redeem us from our evil ways, Jesus won! Christ overcame each person's sin on the cross and then rose again, so that all who lift up their heads and believe in the redemptive work of Christ are forgiven and free to live forgiven and free. However, it is also true that while we get to live free from the penalties of our sin, we're still within swinging range of the sinful blows of others.

Ephesians 6:12 tells us that "we do not wrestle against flesh and blood, but against the rulers, against the authorities, against the cosmic powers over this present darkness, against the spiritual forces of evil in the heavenly places" (ESV). As the devil continues to deceive, fighting for a foothold in people's lives, we must see the ongoing battle with spiritual eyes.

We have a choice each and every day, each time a news headline heralds a heartache. Either we can attempt to answer the hard questions of sin and suffering with the help of Scripture, or we can try to understand them with the help of the news. That's what today's trending news stories hope you'll do. "EXTRA! EXTRA! Read all about it!" But instead of scrolling through newsfeeds, consider reading a different news source first. What we need more than the news is the Good News.

I'm not suggesting you remain ignorant of what is happening in the world. I am simply recommending that you prioritize. When world news shapes your worldview, you will see the Good News in light of the world's darkness. However, if the Good News is your lens, then all of the human suffering, political debates, trashy tabloids, natural disasters, and mass murders will be better understood in the light of His Word.

What we need more than the news is the Good News.

We need to see the world through a biblical lens rather than viewing Scripture through the world's warped spectacles. If you haven't already silenced the news notifications on your phone, stopping the headlines from popping up on your screen, take a moment to go to your phone's settings and do that now. Perhaps you'll keep them hidden rather than front and center when you return to your online resources. Choose to make your primary news source the Word of God, not the words of commentators such as those on CNN or FOX—not for forty days but for all your days. When you know what you believe to be true about God, then you're ready to face the world.

Lord, In light of this present darkness, I'm choosing to keep my eyes on You, the Light of the World. Help me to filter all the bad news through the Good News of Your eternal love. Trying to comprehend Your goodness through the world's sad filter doesn't work. In the always good name of Jesus, Amen.

DAY 30

Little Foxes

Catch for us the foxes,
   the little foxes
that ruin the vineyards,
   our vineyards that are in bloom.

Song of Songs 2:15

We've spent the past few days considering what else distracts us from living a life of devotion to God with the precious people right in front of us. From sweet treats to sweet tea, from a morning cup of coffee to a nightly glass of wine to online games to music and movies and trending news stories . . . these all seem like such small, harmless things. When we give them so much of our time and attention, however, these small things can become massive strongholds in our lives. Consider the actual size of your phone; it's obvious to see that small things can become big things if we're not careful. Much too big and much too consuming.

My phone and laptop and social media sites mean more to me than they should. While they started out as tools that I own, they ended up owning me. What was intended for me to master eventually mastered me. **Fasting from these digital demigods allows me to lay down these little masters in order to focus my life upon the Master.**

I recently heard someone state that high school students today experience more stress at the thought of their phone battery dying than they do when preparing for a job interview. I've seen adults panic at the airport, searching for an outlet to charge their phones before a flight. It's not just the young who struggle today but all of us in this digital era. The big things have become the small things, and the small things are now much too big. We're tied to our stuff, and we can't break loose.

Boundaries around our online world protect our real-life world.

Norwegian author and theologian Ole Hallesby wrote, "The purpose of [fasting] is to loosen to some degree the ties which bind us to the world of material things and our surroundings as a whole, in order that we may concentrate all our spiritual powers upon the unseen and eternal things."[1] Whether you picked up this book with the idea of taking a short break from digital distractions or a permanent one, the purpose of this fast is to break the ties that bind us to our little masters so that we might be freed up to look up and experience the Master. Fasting works like a fence, holding all the little temporary things back so that we might live undistracted, able to enjoy the grandiose, eternal presence of God.

If you've ever grown a garden and placed a fence around your tender greens, you know what I mean when I say that little critters belong outside of the strawberry patch. If they're inside the garden, all is lost. The same is true in our lives. The online world isn't welcome when my family is having dinner or when I'm hanging out with a real-life friend. The online world isn't welcome on my dates with my husband or in our bed. The online world isn't welcome when I'm homeschooling my kids or enjoying some

Sabbath rest. Fasting is a short-term fence, but setting long-term boundaries keeps us safe and secure within our personal garden plots. Boundaries around our online world protect our real-life world. Without boundaries, we bound off after every little notification that pops up all day long! We are unprotected and unaware of the ruin within our reach.

Your life is a precious garden, intended for flourishing fruit, but you have an enemy who loves to eat away at the produce you produce. He loves to slip stealthily into the private plot of your life while you are distracted by other things. That's why it's crucial to use some of your time to consider what you want your life to look like beyond these fasting days. At the end of the fast, I'll share with you some of my own personal boundaries, but in the meantime, I want you to brainstorm some of your own.

In one of the smallest books of the Bible, the Song of Songs, the author paints a beautiful picture of how passionately the Lord pursues us for an intimate relationship with Himself and how we are to love Him back, even if it requires saying no to the love this world offers us. It is in this context that we find today's passage: "Catch for us the foxes, the little foxes that ruin the vineyards, our vineyards that are in bloom" (Song 2:15). Little foxes ruin vineyards. Little things, over time, have the power to ruin big things.

Sometimes, it's the smallest critters that do the most damage within the garden of our lives. We often let them in and let them remain for far too long because they are so small. I know in my marriage, in my mothering, and in my thought life too, the smallest problems have often led to my biggest struggles. Allowing too many nights without clear communication between my husband and me has caused miscommunication and deep wounds. Growing weary of being consistent with my children has allowed them to form bad habits with their homework and household chores. One late-night show turns to binge-watching the entire season. One cup of coffee in the morning suddenly becomes a main source of strength throughout the day. When seemingly small things lead to big things, small distractions lead to big destruction. Over time, with increasing frequency, little foxes make a mess out of our lives.

A person doesn't usually fall out of the habit of daily Bible reading because they miss one day. It's a string of days, all in a row. The same is true when we miss too many Sundays at church. Weekly fellowship, we've already discussed, builds up the body as a whole and strengthens each individual part at the same time. So why do we fall away if it's so good for us? Well, it usually starts small, with a work deadline or a weekend away, perhaps followed by a sore throat or a houseful of guests. One Sunday at a time, and before we know it, our church attendance ceases altogether. Be wary. Guard the garden of your life by keeping the big things the big things and the small things the small things. Keep the Master the master, and don't let the things you own, own you.

> *When seemingly small things lead to big things, small distractions lead to big destruction.*

Nomophobia describes our culture's fear of being separated from our phones. Only about six inches long and three inches wide, weighing in at a mere six ounces, these mini masters threaten to steal our peace. The thought of them dying nearly kills us! One surefire way to discover if a digital demigod (or anything else at all) is still sitting on the throne of your life is to ask yourself these questions: *Would a dead battery kill me? How would I respond to misplacing my phone and having to run errands without it?*

If you couldn't have a cup of coffee for forty days, would you struggle in big ways? Would giving up wine cause you to whine? Would a week without gaming make your real life no fun at all?

Guard the garden of your faith life, your family life, and your real life by recognizing what little foxes have made themselves at home. Little foxes are more than a little distracting.

Master Jesus, I want You to be the biggest thing in my life! But all the little squares on Instagram, and all the minutes I spend scrolling through them, add up and crowd You out—all the little pings and rings drown You out. Coffee offers me strength so I don't turn to You, and entertainment keeps me distracted for hours on end so I don't even notice how far I've strayed. Help me to build a fence around my life, Jesus, before these fasting days are through. I'm asking in Your name, Amen.

DAY 31

Self(ie) Fast

Make it your ambition to lead a quiet life: You should mind your own business and work with your hands, just as we told you, so that your daily life may win the respect of outsiders and so that you will not be dependent on anybody.

1 Thessalonians 4:11–12

Four decades ago, my Sunday school teacher taught me a lesson I've never forgotten. She began by asking all of us children to point to another person in the room. We stuck out our little pointer fingers at one another, giggling. She then remarked that some of us had our thumbs up, but others didn't. "Everybody put up your thumbs, and keep pointing," she said, and then went on. "If you look at your hand now, you'll see that your thumb is pointing straight up, toward God." She gave us the thumbs up sign. "Good job! That's always the most important, because He gets our first love and attention. The next finger is your pointer finger, and it's pointed away from you toward someone else. That's important too, because God told us that if we love Him, we will love others."

My teacher went on to share one more valuable lesson. She told us to look at the other, hidden fingers curled up inside our hands. "Those are the ones pointing back at you. Loving yourself is important, because God thinks you're worth loving, but our self-love is something that should remain quiet and private, not up top and public for everyone else to see."

Living a private life is terribly hard in this very public, self(ie)-obsessed world.

Since we've already talked about loving God first and others second, I want to focus now on this idea of remaining hidden. Living a private life is terribly hard in this very public, self(ie)-obsessed world. We post about ourselves and use filters to make us look even better than we are. However, God isn't impressed with us nearly as much as we're impressed with ourselves. He's not even impressed by the spectacle of our religious lives. Take a look at this passage from Micah 6.

> "With what shall I come before the LORD,
>   and bow myself before God on high?
> Shall I come before him with burnt offerings,
>   with calves a year old?
> Will the LORD be pleased with thousands of rams,
>   with ten thousands of rivers of oil?
> Shall I give my firstborn for my transgression,
>   the fruit of my body for the sin of my soul?"
> He has told you, O man, what is good;
>   and what does the LORD require of you
> but to do justice, and to love kindness,
>   and to walk humbly with your God? (Mic. 6:6–8 ESV)

All God cares about is that we are kind and just toward others as we humbly walk with Him. Nobody else needs to see it. Though Shakespeare said, "All the world's a stage," *The Message* paraphrase of the following passage begins with the subject line, "The World Is Not a Stage."

> Be especially careful when you are trying to be good so that you don't make a performance out of it. It might be good theater, but the God who made you won't be applauding.
>
> When you do something for someone else, don't call attention to yourself. You've seen them in action, I'm sure—"playactors" I call them—treating prayer meeting and street corner alike as a stage, acting compassionate as long as someone is watching, playing to the crowds. They get applause, true, but that's all they get. When you help someone out, don't think about how it looks. Just do it—quietly and unobtrusively. (Matt. 6:1–4)

Humility and unobtrusiveness, though valued by God, are of no value to the world. Conversely, what the world values is of no value to God. That's the rub. He honors the humble and extends intimate friendship to those who are meek, but the world cheers for those who shimmer and shine, who sparkle spectacularly. Thin and beautiful, clever and quotable, wise and winsome, with happy family photos and perfectly plated food. The temptation is to play some likable version of yourself, making a spectacle of moments that were never intended to be public.

Public performance makes private humility hard.

Public performance makes private humility hard. It's impossibly difficult to walk humbly hidden with God and at the same time impress everybody else. And yet, there is an "impressing" that happens as we commit to living our real lives quietly offline. Today's Scripture promises that our daily life may win the respect of outsiders. That's the goal! Not that we win the masses but that we win individuals to the Master.

Not long ago I went on a walk with my friend Jenny, and she told me God had convicted her heart that much of her up-front serving in the church was motivated by an unhealthy need to be seen and affirmed as generous and godly. Today, she frequently asks herself, *Who am I doing this for, Jesus or Jenny?*

Jesus said, "A new command I give you: Love one another. As I have loved you, so you must love one another. By this everyone will know that you are my disciples, if you love one another" (John 13:34–35). **When we are focused on loving God by loving others, not to meet our own need to look good but as an overflow of humble love, people will know who we belong to and will want in on the action!** The focus won't be on us but on Him.

Over the course of the past week, you've been considering what else you might need to lay down in order to pick up the devoted life God has for you. Is it possible that the main thing getting between you and the Lord, and you and others, is . . . you? Are you the common denominator? Is your hunger to be seen getting in the way of you seeing *Him* and *them?* Even when you appear to be serving generously, are you self-serving?

Or maybe you don't serve others at all. Maybe you've simply made a life out of serving yourself. Do you give in to every impulse you have to meet your own needs, express your own thoughts, or satisfy your own hunger but struggle to feel and respond to the needs or wants of others? Do you interrupt others when they talk or forget to give them a chance to talk at all? Do your big emotions, big purchases, and big plans distract you from what others are thinking and feeling and needing? Is it possible that you need a "self fast"? A time of laying aside your self-interest, self-centeredness, and self-love?

I don't know what this will look like in your life, but I have ideas about how it needs to look in mine. During my fasting days, I sense the Lord calling me to talk about myself less. As I take a break from posting selfies online, I am trying to also take a break from talking about myself to every real-life person who crosses my path.

As we fast from posting about ourselves, let's commit to loving God and loving others, and keep the self-love smaller and quieter—more private, less public.

Dear Lord, Help me to quit my self-focus. No more of this selfie life; I want my focus on You and others—for Your glory and their good!

In Jesus's generous name, for He came to serve and not be served, Amen.

DAY 32

Fasting from Fighting

A gentle answer turns away wrath,
but a harsh word stirs up anger.

Proverbs 15:1

Sometimes my youngest son, Asher, has water polo tournaments that stretch from Friday through Sunday. As a
churchgoing family, my husband and I have prayed long
and hard about what we should do on those occasions. For the
first fifteen years, we took a firm "no sports on Sundays" stance,
but then Asher began to dream of playing water polo collegiately.
We continued to pray, and although we believe in honoring the
Sabbath and value consistent Christian fellowship, we felt the Lord
lead us to sign our son up for a handful of tournaments each year.

While the specific reasons for our choice aren't the point of
today's reading, I don't mind sharing a few of them: we get together
with other believers multiple times throughout the week, so we're
not in danger of giving up that habit; we're in the Word as a family
almost daily; and Asher is also part of a small group Bible study.
What's more, we believe Jesus modeled pulling away in order to

experience Sabbath rest for the purpose of intimacy and renewal with the Father on a daily basis, not just on the seventh day. Finally, on these occasional Sundays, my husband takes the rest of the family to church and Asher and I "do church" together on the road. Some of the most incredible times I've had in the Word with this particular child have been on our way to tournaments on Sunday mornings.

With a Bible in his hands and a steering wheel in mine, we dig into the Scriptures. We discuss what it means for Asher to be Christ's ambassador to his team and how God might use him to influence his teammates for Christ. We worship the Lord through song and pray for each teammate by name. By the time we walk onto the pool deck, my kid is already wet with living water.

One Sunday, Asher pulled such deep insights from our Bible reading that I shared his words on social media, along with the Scripture reference and a picture of him jumping into the pool. It was a darling picture and a meaningful post. When the game started, I gave my full attention to cheering on the team and connecting with other parents. An hour later, as the kids scrambled from the pool, I looked online and found that a heated debate had erupted in the comment thread of my post. One woman in particular was offended I had posted so shamelessly about missing church, and others had jumped to my defense.

Shocked by her tone, I doubted she had even read the entire post, considered the Scripture for herself, or prayed through how she might speak (her) truth to me in love. Her angry response had nothing to

Christians are allowed to disagree with one another in a loving way.

do with my Facebook message, only the fact that Asher and I hadn't received our message from a pastor that morning.

Why am I sharing this, knowing that some of you will disagree with our decision to let our child compete on these rare Sunday mornings? That's exactly why! My point is this: Christians are allowed to disagree with one another in a loving way. If we can't be loving toward one another, how will we learn to disagree in a loving manner with those who don't share our faith?

If a gentle answer has the power to turn away wrath (Prov. 15:1), I believe a gentle comment in an angry thread is able to do the same. Though I was shaken by this woman's response to my post, I quickly closed my phone and prayed. I prayed as I poured lemonade for the team. I prayed as I high-fived my kid and listened to the coach give the boys feedback. Once my son was settled in the shade with his teammates, awaiting their next game, I found a quiet place to thoughtfully respond.

To the woman I wrote, "I'm sorry that this was so stressful for you to read. It is never my desire to be a stumbling block to others. I will consider your words as I continue to take the matter to the Lord." Then I powered down my phone and powered up my prayer life. I prayed for the offended woman to know the peace and presence of our Savior's love so radically that she couldn't help but be more loving herself. I also invited the Lord to speak to me about the matter. If God wanted to convict me, I was open to conviction, though I knew it wasn't like Him to speak to my soft heart through the loveless words of an angry voice online.

God did speak to my heart that day, and in the days that followed. I sensed Him telling me to fast from social media on Sundays. (We'll talk more about this in a coming chapter.) But the main thing God communicated to my heart was that He wanted me to fast from fighting, not for just forty days but for three hundred and sixty-five days a year. I'm learning to lean lovingly into conflict when the Lord (and not my emotions) prompts me, without engaging in a fight. Sometimes a gentle answer is all that's needed to subdue another's anger or criticism, and other times I merely take down a post that wasn't well received.

People will be offended by us, whether on Facebook or face-to-face, and some of that we have control over. Not being offensive helps. Humbly consider how your words might be received by others before you speak them or type them. And when you do offend others, because sometimes you will, "Be quick to listen, slow to speak and slow to become angry, because human anger does not produce the righteousness that God desires" (James 1:19–20). With the Lord's help, we can be peacemakers rather than troublemakers online. As you continue to fast from social media short-term, consider how you might fast from online fights long-term once you return to the online conversation.

While you cannot control the offensive behavior of others, you can choose whether to respond offensively.

People say things online that they would never say in person. If you have family members or friends who love to challenge views that are different from their own—about faith, politics, or whatever—commit to staying calm and kind. Rather than jumping into the ring, swinging back with your own hot words, take this Scripture to heart:

> Run away from infantile indulgence. Run after mature righteousness—faith, love, peace—joining those who are in honest and serious prayer before God. Refuse to get involved in inane discussions; they always end up in fights. God's servant must not be argumentative, but a gentle listener and a teacher who keeps cool, working firmly but patiently with those who refuse to obey. (2 Tim. 2:22–23 MSG)

While you cannot control the offensive behavior of others, you can choose whether to respond offensively. That choice is yours and yours alone. **Make the choice today to respond gently.** Romans 14:1 says, "Welcome with open arms fellow believers who don't see things the way you do. And don't jump all over them every time they do or say something you don't agree with—even when it seems that they are strong on opinions but weak in the faith" (MSG).

Dear Lord, The result of spending time with You is that I become more like You. Not only is Your peace and self-control available to me but so is Your gentle nature. When others want to fight, I don't have to fight back. Make me an ambassador of Your peace wherever I go, online and off. Make me a peacemaker, not a troublemaker.

I pray all this in the peaceful name of Jesus, Amen.

DAY 33

Holy Habits

Discipline yourself for the purpose of godliness.

1 Timothy 4:7 NASB

My children were young when I recognized some bad habits creeping into my life. Nothing terribly sinful by the world's standards, perhaps, but I was growing weary from sleep deprivation and lazy from lack of accountability. Though I never meant to let things into my life that would distract me from my faith or family, I realized that without good habits I wouldn't be able to keep my priorities in place.

But more than good habits, I needed godly habits—holy habits. One day, as the children napped, I sat down with a pad of paper to write a list of the things I wanted to do and the boundaries I needed to set for myself. The list went something like this:

Thank God at the start of each day.

Read my Bible and pray.

Speak positive words.

Sit down to breakfast as a family.

Read to my children.

Sing to them.

Do crafts.

Take them to the park.

Pray for the kids out loud in the car.

Pray for the kids as I do laundry.

Try a new recipe each week.

Write a note to a friend each week.

Go to bed with my husband each night.

Don't complain.

Forgive quickly.

Don't run to sugar or alcohol to cope with stress.

Don't turn to TV or Facebook to cope with stress either.

I can see myself sitting at the kitchen table that day, looking at the "craft cupboard" door slightly ajar because it was too jam-packed with fun supplies to close completely. Sticker books and puzzles were shoved in there too. *Little Men, Charlotte's Web*, and the *Children's Storybook Bible* were on a small table in the corner of our kitchen nook. I was already doing many of the things I wrote on my list, but other things were going to take intentional, purposeful work. I don't recall how many days or months passed before I set that list to verse, but eventually I did. I titled my poem "Holy Habits."

> *Only shop when there's something I need. But more than good habits I needed godly habits— holy habits.*

First thing in the morning, when the dark sky's turning light,
I wake up and I whisper, "Thank you, God, for my sweet
    night."
I crawl out from my covers and trod to the kitchen where
I see my faithful Bible sitting on the table there.

My teapot's ready-waiting to make the water sing,
So I start the kettle heating and before my King I bring
My prayers and petitions, my praises and my fears,
And by the time the water's hot, I feel His presence near.

When my time with Him has ended, I go to gently rouse
My family from their slumber, then I serve my breakfast
    crowd.
Once we've cleared the dishes, and every child has said
    "Thanks, Mom!"
I send them to their bedrooms to get their school clothes on.

The taxi shuttle (that's my van) takes us everywhere.
It's broken down a time or two, but most often gets us
    there.
At the curb we pray together, before they jump outside.
Days are hard on little ones, so I ask God to be on their side.

Now before I continue, I've simply got to say
These things I do aren't natural, I just practice them every
    day.
I used to wake and groan, "Oh, my back, it hurts even after
    my rest";
But I noticed that those first words colored my day with a
    verbal mess.

So listen to this story with ears purposed to hear what I say.
I'm not better than you, I just made habits that promote a
    holier day.
Holiness isn't natural; selfishness, entitlement, strife
Are the things that come more easily to this honest mom
    and wife.

So back to my day and the choices I make, I hope that you'll
listen up.
If choices aren't made purposefully, I guarantee you're
going to get stuck:
Stuck on the couch eating cookie dough or scrolling
through your phone;
Sneaking onto the porch with a glass of wine, because you
long for time alone.

During the hours it's just the kids and me, with my husband
working and gone,
I keep my hands busy with hard work—Proverbs 31 says
they ought to be strong.
I make an effort to avoid the traps that so easily lure us away,
TV shows and computer screens, when there are children
who want me to play.

I purposed to try new recipes and hit the gym a time or
two,
And I purposed to send an encouraging note every
afternoon.
I purposed to meet my husband at the door each night with
a kiss,
And go to bed when he goes to bed, because beds weren't
just made for rest.

I purposed to pray as I fold the laundry, for the hearts that
fill each shirt,
That they come to know Jesus Christ and are protected
from getting hurt.
I purposed to not go shopping unless we truly have a need,
I know my tendency to spend; it's a conviction I must heed.

I started with a deliberate plan and worked intentionally
Because holy lives don't follow the culture; they don't come
naturally.

Eventually my plans became my habits, and that's now
what makes up my life.
I told you before, and I'll tell you again, I'm just a simple
mom and wife.

I didn't include this imperfectly metered poem because it's good but because it perfectly captures my commitment to discipline myself. With God's help, godliness is possible. This poem isn't simply about parenting; the application is the same for us all. Holy lives don't just happen, and they don't come naturally. We must make intentional choices and ask God for His help if we want to grow up in our faith.

Most of us signed up for this forty-day social media fast because we recognized a lack of discipline in our online lives. So, over the next few days, in an effort to become more self-disciplined, let's turn to the spiritual disciplines. Spiritual disciplines are the holy habits taught and modeled for us in the Bible. When we practice them regularly, we grow spiritually. My poetic list included a few, such as spending time in the Word, fellowshipping with other believers, and having a consistent prayer life. In the chapters ahead, we'll consider those disciplines, along with a few others.

Because there are many tempting distractions in this world luring us away from Christlikeness, we must be spiritually strong. The problem is we just aren't—which is why we need an exercise plan to build our underutilized faith muscles. The spiritual disciplines of the Christian life work to make us stronger and more self-controlled.

Today, practicing any discipline is harder than ever, not because there are more distractions (though I believe there are) but because we live in a world that doesn't value self-discipline or hard work and promotes ease and comfort. As Andy Crouch wrote, "Because technology is devoted primarily to making our lives easier, it discourages us from disciplines, especially ones that involve disentangling ourselves from technology itself."[1]

Having disentangled yourself from technology, now is the time to put some effort into practicing these holy habits so that you will live a holy, devoted life. Exchanging distraction for devotion won't happen by accident, but it can happen on purpose. It doesn't happen naturally, but it can happen supernaturally.

Exchanging distraction for devotion won't happen by accident, but it can happen on purpose.

Take some time today to write out a list of the habits you want to fit into your busy life, things you've been too distracted or undisciplined to do. Include those things you need to stop doing as well. Without a plan, nothing's going to change, but with a good plan, and the help of a good God, change is possible.

Grab a prayer journal or a piece of paper and write out a few of the holy habits you want to develop in the days ahead.

Dear Lord, My natural tendencies need Your supernatural help. I'm ready to make some holier habits. I know that with You, this is possible. Thank You and Amen.

DAY 34

Shabbat Shalom

The Spiritual Discipline of Sabbath Rest

> By the seventh day God had finished the work he had
> been doing; so on the seventh day he rested from all
> his work. Then God blessed the seventh day and made
> it holy, because on it he rested from all the work of
> creating that he had done.
>
> Genesis 2:2–3

Y ou can't know someone unless you spend time with them; likewise, you can't know the power and peace of God if you don't spend time with the person of Christ. It's hard to invest in any relationship when we're always on the run. Whether we're running to our job or running from one form of entertainment to another, it's only in the moments when we cease from running that we get to know God.

From the beginning, God made our rest a priority. There's no denying it. The spiritual discipline of rest is woven throughout the entire tapestry of Scripture, from the creation story, where He set aside the seventh day for us to rest (Gen. 2:2–3), to the giving of the Ten Commandments, where our rest became more than a mere suggestion (Exod. 20:8), to the example of Christ Himself, where He pulled away and invited His disciples to do the same (Mark 6:21). But if rest is so essential, why is it so hard? Why does the thought of taking a break threaten to break us when rest is what remakes, renews, restores, and re-creates us?

Every generation has found it terribly difficult to cease from striving. I daresay that today, in our ever-connected culture, connecting to God in a quiet, restful way is harder than ever. There is always work to be done, emails to respond to, and a phone to answer. Even when we leave work, we take work with us.

God has so much more to give us than one phone-free hour of fellowship on Sunday mornings. A week of pouring out requires more than an hour of being poured back into. If you've experienced a fresh filling of His power since you began this fast from online distractions, maybe you ought to consider setting down your phone every Sunday, even after your fast comes to an end. **Consider each Sabbath day a fasting day. A day to fast from work in order to rest, and to fast from constant connectedness with the world in order to connect with the One who made the world.** Fasting is the key to Sabbath rest.

Fasting is the key to Sabbath rest.

I was a sophomore in college the first time I felt convicted to observe the Sabbath. Though I was raised in a Christian home and had memorized the Ten Commandments as a child, I don't have a single memory of being taught what honoring the Sabbath was supposed to look like. A decade after I hid the Ten Commandments in my heart, I decided that I would do all of my homework for the weekend on Saturdays so I could rest on Sundays. I got into the practice of driving an hour to the nearest beach after church on Sunday mornings. After parking, I'd go for a long walk. Though I didn't have a phone in my pocket, I did have my bright yellow

Walkman. I'd make it back to campus by dinnertime, visit the cafeteria, and go to bed early.

As a direct result of honoring the Sabbath, my friendship with the Lord of the Sabbath grew. And that's really what the discipline of Sabbath rest is about. We fast from work in order to find our rest in Him. We fast from striving in order to experience His divine abiding.

Work, however, isn't the only distraction threatening us on Sundays. We're a nation obsessed with fun. We sometimes call our play recreation, but *recreation* is a funny word. Synonymous with *play*, *recreation* is formed by placing the preface *re* before the root word *create*: meaning to create again or make new.

While playing is good for us and has the power to fill us up in many ways, I have to disagree with those who say that it holds the power to re-create us. Nothing renews our physical or spiritual health like rest does. Re-creating requires not playing but resting.

Whether you're running on Sundays to get your work done or running to get your fun in, the invitation is the same. **God invites us to fast from running and find our rest.** The Lord loves us so much that He wants to be with us, *re-creating* us from the inside out, but this requires us to accept His invitation and slow down. Fasting can help us do just that. When we discipline ourselves to lay down all distractions—work, food, music, studying, social media, phone calls, Snapchat, Netflix, Instagram—there's a chance we can learn to lay our body down too.

For thousands of years, since God rested on the seventh day of creation, the seventh day of the week has remained His in many parts of the world. The Jews were the first to receive and obey this command. From sundown on Friday to sundown on Saturday night, they greet one another with the words, "*Shabbat Shalom*," which translates to "Sabbath peace." This is spoken as a blessing upon those who respond to God's invitation to rest. *Shabbat Shalom*: May the peace that comes from observing the Sabbath be yours today. Oh, what a blessing and invitation. "Be still, and know that I am God" (Ps. 46:10).

For those who struggle to slow down and rest, the spiritual discipline of fasting can help you become more disciplined in honoring the sabbath. Sometimes you need to go fast in order to slow down.

Fast from running and trying so hard. One day a week, find your peace in the presence of God. If there are other ways you might fast on Sundays in order to feast on Him, consider those as well. Cease from eating compulsively and know the filling of God. Turn off your TV show and let Him show you Himself. Go for a few weeks without dating or hanging out with friends on Sunday nights and invest in the intimate friendship available to you in Christ. Stop shopping and know that He is all you need. Cease filling yourself up with temporary pleasures and pursuits and quietly avail yourself of His eternal filling. Take a break from everything that distracts and devote yourself to knowing Him.

When we step back from this world's priorities and prioritize our rest in Him, we can find peace every day of the week. Those who lack peace are often restless. But those who find rest also find peace.

Those who lack peace are often restless. But those who find rest also find peace.

Remember Psalm 23, where the good Shepherd "makes [us] lie down" (v. 2)? Well, you actually have the freedom to choose if you're going to lie down or not. Choose to accept this gracious invitation and prioritize rest for the rest of this fast, then consider what your Sabbaths might look like beyond your fasting days. Perhaps you need an ongoing phone fast every Sunday so that you might receive the blessing: *Shabbat Shalom.*

Lord of the Sabbath, Help me to honor You by obeying You. Teach me how fasting relates to resting. I am willing to lay down my work, play, phone . . . whatever it takes to experience Your peace, power, and presence in my life. Thank You for being God; I long to be still long enough to know You better. Amen.

DAY 35

Dress Rehearsal

The Spiritual Discipline of Prayer

And when you pray, do not be like the hypocrites, for they love to pray standing in the synagogues and on the street corners to be seen by others. Truly I tell you, they have received their reward in full. But when you pray, go into your room, close the door and pray to your Father, who is unseen. Then your Father, who sees what is done in secret, will reward you.

Matthew 6:5-6

As I prepared for my first social media fast, I chose to bring along two books as literary companions. Both of them focused on the power of prayer. In recent years, I'd been too distracted to devote myself to prayer and was eager for a revival in my heart and in my home. Leonard Ravenhill's classic *Why Revival Tarries*, challenged me from its opening lines:

The Cinderella of the church of today is the prayer meeting. This handmaid of the Lord is unloved and unwooed because she is not dripping with the pearls of intellectualism, nor glamorous with the silks of philosophy; neither is she enchanting with the tiara of psychology. She wears the homespuns of sincerity and humility and so is not afraid to kneel![1]

Unfortunately, for the majority of the year, talking with God takes a back seat in my life because I'm too busy talking with everyone else. I get distracted and I forget. However, when I fast, I remember. When I take a break from the constant chatter online, I am reminded how desperate I am for the most important conversation of all.

The last couple of days, we have shifted our focus to the spiritual disciplines and to intentionally exercising our underutilized spiritual muscles. **If our prayer life has atrophied from underuse this past decade, we can use the time we have freed up during this fast to flex our prayer muscles again.** Since we're offline, we won't be tempted to do it in a way that will be seen or liked by others. Quietly, in our private places of prayer, we can humbly engage with God again, not only for our own benefit but on behalf of others. When our heads are bowed before the Lord and not our screens, revelation and transformation pour into our lives and into the lives of those we're interceding for.

My grandpa regularly told me, "Your grandma and I are praying for you, Wendy. We pray specifically that you know the joy of a Christian marriage." I don't remember him sharing any other prayers. Though Grandpa and Grandma passed away quite a few years ago, their intercessory prayers live on today in my marriage. Regularly, I look at my husband and find myself overwhelmed by the kindness of the Lord. I thank God not only for my husband but also for my grandpa and grandma and their prayers.

During my annual social media fasts, I use much of my time and energy to pray for my own children. I mentioned at the start of this chapter that two books on prayer have helped me grow stronger and more consistent in my prayer life. The first is Ravenhill's *Why Revival Tarries*, and the second is *Praying the Scriptures for Your Teens* by Jodie Berndt. Each day, with the help of stories and Scriptures, Berndt led me in prayer for my three boys. I prayed they would be truth tellers and have integrity; I prayed they would be servants and not self-seeking; I prayed against depression and rebellion and self-injury; I prayed for their future spouses.

Fast from your online conversation in order to engage in a heavenly one.

When Matt and I got married, the first book I read was *The Power of a Praying Wife* by Stormie Omartian.[2] One day, he left for work upset about something, though I had no idea what. Since we had dated long-distance and for only a few months before we got married, I didn't know him well. I opened *The Power of a Praying Wife* and prayed the Scripture-based prayer about anger. That afternoon Matt came home early and sat at the kitchen table as I prepped dinner. He put his head in his hands and groaned, "I was so angry today. I can see that now, but I don't know why."

The next day after he left for work, I was moved again to pray, this time through the chapter on pride. Again he came home overwhelmed by a clear conviction. He told me, "I realized as I was driving to work this morning that I struggle with anger because I struggle with pride."

I was shocked how quickly the Lord was moving through my simple prayers, and I remember praying that night, *Lord, if prayer really works, I don't ever want to stop praying!* Eventually, however, I did. Prayer takes self-control; that's why it's one of the spiritual disciplines. **Staying devoted to prayer is hard when you're distracted.** My online life has certainly hindered my prayer life.

Andrew Bonar once said, "Fasting is abstaining from anything that hinders prayer."[3] This is one of the main benefits of fasting from social media as far as I am concerned.

Let's not fast from social media in order to free up more time to read good books (though I do hope you are being blessed by this one). This is one of the main benefits of fasting from social media as far as I am concerned.

As long as we are here on earth, this sort of dialogue with God will take discipline. I've said before that online chatter is loud and distracting, but a time is coming, and fast approaching, when the online world and the rest of this world will pass away. At that time, we will find ourselves standing before the Lord, like Cinderella before her prince. The eternal chorus of our dance will be, "Worthy is the Lamb, who was slain, to receive power and wealth and wisdom and strength and honor and glory and praise!" (Rev. 5:12). A day is coming when all other songs will cease and this one will echo on for eternity.

Years ago, a man leading worship at our church asked us to stand and sing this with invitation: "This is your dress rehearsal. A day will come when you will begin your forever life in God's presence, singing His praises. Let's get ready for that glorious day." I know that this chapter is about prayer, not singing, but the overarching theme is the same. We are communicating with the Lamb who was slain, the One who died for our sins so that we might have access to His presence both now and forevermore! What an incredible thought: we are able to speak with Him and sing to Him now.

It takes spiritual discipline to put down your phone and get down on your knees.

Consider these forty days your dress rehearsal. It takes spiritual discipline to put down your phone and get down on your knees, but on the other side of this life awaits another, where kneeling won't take any discipline at all. You will do it supernaturally— standing, kneeling, dancing, and singing in the presence of the Lamb. Glory!

Dear Lord, Thank You for giving me a way to communicate with You today—privately and prayerfully. It's a humble, unseen practice that won't get me "likes" online, but it's the conversation I'm most desperate for. Thank You also for the opportunity to pray for those I know and love. Impress Your will for them upon my heart and drive me to my knees on their behalf. What a privilege it is to talk with You, in Jesus's name. Amen.

Spiritually Disciplined vs. Self-Disciplined

Perhaps you made the decision to fast from social media because you lack self-discipline in your time online. "Just one more episode" turns into three more episodes of your favorite show. Setting your alarm for tomorrow morning rolls into an hour scrolling through news feeds and YouTube videos. Practicing these spiritual disciplines won't only help you grow more spiritually disciplined but self-disciplined too. Keep exercising your spiritual muscles, and you'll grow stronger in every area of your life.

DAY 36

Take Me to Church

The Spiritual Discipline of Going to Church

Oh, magnify the LORD with me,
and let us exalt his name together!
Psalm 34:3 ESV

In 2019 I received a private message from a woman named Lauren who had seen a graphic on Instagram inviting her to join one of my annual sugar fasts. Lauren wrote, "Hi, Wendy, I found your challenge and am following along. I'm not Christian but not against trying your way." She went on to ask me how to use a Bible to look up the verses each day. We had a meaningful exchange, but then I didn't hear from her again until after the fast, when she sent me another note. "Thank you so much. Doing the 40-Day Sugar Fast helped me to realize that I need a relationship with God." She went on to say that those forty days of prayer and fasting had changed her present life *and her eternal life*. And to think, she came across that invitation on Instagram.

I'm amazed how God actively blesses people through the internet. He's always pursued us right where we are. **Just as Jesus came to earth two thousand years ago, today He's pursuing people through the posts of gospel-minded men and women.** He's using His people on the internet because that's where most people are "living" today.

Social media is our current culture's "city gate"—the place where prominent people gathered to talk and conduct business during ancient times (see Prov. 31:23). If they had an important matter to discuss, they'd meet and debate it at the gates of the city. Today, people congregate online. If you are trying to gain access into the lives of others, whether you're wanting to make friends or influence people, social media is a powerful tool.

Just recently I heard Beth Moore talking about using Twitter in this gospel-centered way. While there is power there, Beth warned, "Being on there doesn't mean being on there all the time."[1] Unfortunately, many people open a social media account innocently enough, but over time it becomes an unhealthy obsession. Salvation power is alive and well online today—but for us to remain aflame, we must keep feeding the flame. One of the best ways I know to do that is by practicing this next spiritual discipline: going to church. A brick and mortar place of worship.

Back in the ancient era of literal city gates there was another place where God's people gathered: the synagogue. When Jesus and His disciples would arrive at a new town, they would go to the local synagogue to share the mystery of God's kingdom with others. This was His custom. It's what He did regularly. Matthew 4:23 tells us that "Jesus went throughout Galilee, teaching in their synagogues, proclaiming the good news of the kingdom, and healing every disease and sickness among the people." Mark 3:1 (ESV) begins, "Again he entered the synagogue," and we're told in Luke 4:16 that when Jesus arrived in Nazareth, He went to the synagogue on the Sabbath "as was His custom." There's a lesson for us here: going regularly to the house of God must be our *custom*.

Time online, no matter how spiritually enriching it might be for us or others, pales in comparison to attending a healthy church. Before we go out to be the church in this world, we must first go to our local church.

Make sure you spend more time passing through the real church gates than you do linking over to the virtual city gates.

When you get plugged in to a healthy, loving church, serving and being served by real people, your time online becomes a powerful overflow of the love you've received. The right words flow out via text or through a tweet because His Word first flowed in through good Bible teaching. His love flows out of you to the online people you want to influence most powerfully after His love flows into you—powerfully—through a real-life, living, breathing church family. Pouring out without being poured into can lead to burnout. When you burn out, the flame usually goes out, so make sure you spend more time passing through the *real* church gates than you do linking over to the virtual city gates.

If you receive all of your Bible teaching online, it's time to find a home church with real people who can put their arms around you when you're hurting. You need people who will bring you meals when you're grieving and clap their hands when you're celebrating. Though there is power in an online invitation, there's nothing more powerful than one flesh-and-blood person inviting another to lunch and a neighborhood walk or a Bible study with real-life people opening Bibles with real pages and passing real highlighters and Kleenex around a table.

When we spend less time congregating at the digital gates and more time congregating as a congregation, our time online holds

gospel power. The word *congregation* comes from the Greek *ekklesia*. *Ekklesia* is comprised of two words. First, *ek*, which is a preposition meaning "out of," followed by the verb *kaleo*, which means "to call." The purpose of the congregation is literally "to call out."[2]

That's our goal: to call out to those who are in darkness and invite them into the marvelous light of the Son we know and love. Before you plug in to your online life again, make sure you're plugged in to your local *ekklesia*, your congregation. Before you *go out*, it's crucial to be learning and growing together with those who have already been called out. Devote yourself to this spiritual discipline and watch your devotion to the Lord and His people grow!

Devote yourself to learning and growing together and watch your devotion to the Lord and His people grow!

Have you been out of fellowship with the church? Too busy with life or too hurt by the legalism you experienced growing up? Let me invite you back into the fellowship of the church family. As with all families, there is often dysfunction. But the Father of the family, and the Son, are perfect and are calling out to each family member to be perfected in fellowship. You've been digitally unplugged for nearly forty days. As your fast comes to an end, make sure you plug in to a church family of your own.

Lord, You sent Your Son to chase me down; that's why He came down. He found me right where I live. It is now my joy and my job to reach out to others, where they are, whether online or in line behind me at the grocery store. Before I can do that in a healthy way, I need to be part of a healthy church family. Before I can pour out, I need to be poured into. Lead me to a church where I can grow! Show me how I can serve there too. From that healthy, overflowing place, make me a bright light in every city gate I walk through! In Jesus's name, Amen.

DAY 37

Going Dark

The Spiritual Discipline of Reading Your Bible

Your word is a lamp to my feet
and a light to my path.

Psalm 119:105 ESV

*W*hen I started looking at colleges, two in Illinois topped my list. My dad, a graduate of Wheaton College in Illinois, warned me that in that region of the country, the sun doesn't peek through the dark curtain of clouds for three months straight some winters. This California girl decided not to move there for both physical and mental health reasons. Vitamin D has always been good for me emotionally. Years later, my husband was working in the pharmaceutical industry selling psychotropics, and he told me that states with longer winters have higher percentages of residents on antidepressant medications, while those states with the most sun have some of the lowest number of cases per capita. There is something to be said about the power of the sun.

As a Christ follower, I know that there's also tremendous power in the presence of the Son. I actively turn to the Son daily, especially during my own personal dark seasons. During these dark times I struggle to experience His light-bright presence. **When the One who called Himself the Light of the World seems most dim, I have to practice the spiritual discipline of opening up His Word.** Believing what it says, even if it contradicts how I feel, has been one of the greatest boosts to my spiritual health. Jesus's red-letter words tell me the truth about the spiritual darkness that threatens and how I am to remain in His light regardless of my emotions or circumstances.

Jesus promised, "I am the light of the world. Whoever follows me will not walk in darkness, but will have the light of life" (John 8:12 ESV). Remaining close to the Light of the World must be our go-to answer in every dark season. The light of His Word illuminates the dark recesses of our muddled minds and soothes our frightened feelings. The truth of His Word brings us back to the Son-drenched place where we can see clearly and determine where to place our next steps.

Remaining close to the Light of the World must be our go-to answer in every dark season.

Unfortunately, sometimes I settle for the pixelated glow of my phone rather than the "light of life" I'm promised when I walk with Christ. Just the other night, I was tossing and turning in bed, sleepless and anxious with a nagging cough and nagging worries too. At 1:37 in the morning, I confused the light of my phone for the Light I needed most. I knew I was struggling physically and emotionally, but instead of turning to the Lord in His Word, I pulled back the covers and quietly went to get my phone in the other room. Ever so lightly, I touched the little square that opened up my Instagram feed. The first graphic that caught my eye consisted of this simple black text on a white backdrop: "I hate to think of the times God has wanted to speak to me but I was too busy looking at someone's vacation pictures on Instagram."[1]

Immediately convicted of having turned on the wrong light, I closed Instagram and opened my Bible app to where I had left off the day before. The light that spilled from the Word of God was just what I needed to displace the darkness that threatened. Though God used that timely Instagram post, it wasn't going to help me. I needed to hear from God Himself.

Many people say that Bible reading is one of the hardest disciplines to practice. They're too distracted by the world to open up the Word with any regularity. In our home we have a saying: "The Word before the world." I have disciplined myself to open my Bible every day before I open my email or social media accounts, and I'm teaching my kids to do the same.

This world can be dark and confusing, but darkness is merely the absence of light. Opening the Bible is like turning on floodlights. We have the most powerful torchlight possible sitting right on our bedside tables. Psalm 119:105 says, "Your word is a lamp to my feet and a light to my path" (ESV). A few verses later we read, "The unfolding of your words gives light; it gives understanding to the simple" (v. 130). The opening passage of this same psalm begins, "You're blessed when you stay on course, walking steadily on the road revealed by GOD" (v. 1 MSG).

It's hard to stay on the road revealed by God when we can't see where to plant our next step. I don't know about you, but I've walked in literal darkness, and I've walked in spiritual darkness as well. God's Word tells us that when we walk with Him, side by side in the light of His Word, we don't need to stumble another day. I'm reminded of the opening verse to the old hymn "Trust and Obey."

When we walk with the Lord
In the light of His Word,
What a glory He sheds on our way.[2]

It takes discipline to pick up the Bible and turn its light on ourselves and our circumstances. But we must intentionally counter the darkness around us and in us by walking with Christ, the Light of the World, and with the counsel of His lamplight. Open His Word today. My daily commentary is not enough to light your life—open His Word and let it shine brightly. Open it up and open your life up to His illuminating presence. Then do it again tomorrow and the next day and the next. Devote yourself to this discipline, without digital distractions. And then, when your fasting days come to an end, keep up this spiritual practice.

Sometimes you have to "go dark" in order to experience the Light of the World.

Make "the Word before the world" your morning mantra.

Sometimes you have to "go dark" in order to experience the Light of the World. That's what you're doing during these fasting days—unplugging from the world in order to plug in to the Light of the World.

Light of the World, When darkness threatens to undo me, when I don't know the answer and have lost my way, You're the Light I need. You're better than vitamin D and better than the glow of my screen in the middle of the night. You're the answer to every dark feeling, thought, and circumstance. I believe it. Tether me to Your side, Lord, that I might never walk in darkness again. And give me the spiritual discipline to remain there.

Shine, Lord Jesus, that I might not stumble another day. In Your light-bright and glorious name, Amen.

DAY 38

The Store vs. His Storehouse

The Spiritual Disciplines of Serving and Tithing

"Bring the whole tithe into the storehouse, so that there may be food in My house, and test Me now in this," says the Lord of hosts, "if I will not open for you the windows of heaven and pour out for you a blessing until it overflows."

Malachi 3:10 NASB

*I*n the opening pages of this book, I mentioned that when we look up there's a chance we'll actually see the real-life people around us. Of course, we don't just want to look up and see them; we want to help meet their needs! The Lord has generously seen and responded to our needs, and we are invited to pass on the love we've been given by seeing, responding to, and caring for others. In this self-centered world, this doesn't come naturally. We have to flex our giving muscles if we want them to be strong.

Today we are considering the spiritual disciplines of serving and tithing—for the two go hand in generous hand. Tithing to the church and supporting other mercy ministries in order to meet the spiritual and practical needs of people locally and globally is one of the clear callings on the Christian life. So is giving the limited resources of your time and talents in the form of actively serving. Unfortunately, loving Christ doesn't magically make us Christlike. We have to practice His generosity as we practice His selflessness and the sacrificial love He modeled for us.

If you struggle with fear at the thought of giving your money to the church, you're not alone. It is hard to give financially to others when all your money barely meets your own needs. The same is true with your time and your energy. But God's Word promises that we don't need to worry. "'Bring the whole tithe into the storehouse, so that there may be food in My house, and test Me now in this,' says the LORD of hosts, 'if I will not open for you the windows of heaven and pour out for you a blessing until it overflows'" (Mal. 3:10 NASB).

I know firsthand that God is true to His Word. I was raised by a single mom who rarely had extra; however, for every ten dollars she earned, my mom placed one back in the offering plate. When I started waiting tables, I did the same. I kept all of my tips in a white envelope and wrote on the outside of it how much money I had made each shift. At the end of the month I made one lump sum deposit into my bank account to pay my bills but held back 10 percent for my tithe. The amount was so small I often tried to justify how the Lord didn't need my meager offering. But over the years, I came to realize that I needed to give more than the Lord needed to receive. I discovered the joy that comes from obeying God and from thinking of myself less and others more. I could see God at work throughout the world, rather than seeing the world only through the oppressive angst of thinking entirely about myself.

Though we think we'll find what we need at the store, God says His storehouse is where abundant blessings flow. When we stop giving only to ourselves and start giving our time and money back to God for the benefit of others, we discover that He has more to give us than we could ever imagine. I'm not talking about paying us back with interest. God loves to give a spiritual return on our spiritual investments—but it starts with the spiritual disciplines of serving and tithing.

Jesus said in Matthew 6:19–20, "Do not store up for yourselves treasures on earth. . . . But store up for yourselves treasures in heaven." Do not limit yourself to what can be found at the store (or on Amazon Prime) but discover what God has *in store* for those whose treasures are stored in heaven. During the last days of this social media fast, exercise the muscles of your faith by making a commitment to tithe and serve.

Traditionally, we practice these disciplines within our local church. We hold babies in the nursery, lead a small group during a midweek Bible study, or serve on the worship team, then give 10 percent of our income to support the ongoing work of ministry in our community and throughout the world.

He knows our needs and promises to meet them when we keep our eyes on Him.

While we are not under the Old Testament law anymore, the Old Testament paints a generous picture of offering for us. Theirs wasn't a simple 10 percent off the top, placed in an offering dish once a year at harvest time. The Israelites gave many different types of offerings, in the temple and at their festivals, all year long. The percentage they gave ended up being far greater than 10 percent, which is why I like to consider 10 percent a good starting point!

Instead of asking God how you could possibly give 10 percent, ask Him what percentage He wants you to give and start there. My guess is that the number will be higher than you imagine. I've heard of people who started with the typical 10 percent, and every year that God provided for their needs they increased their giving another percentage point. Year after year after year!

While most people choose to give all of their tithe directly to their local church, others feel led to give a portion to missionaries they know personally. Again, I encourage you to ask God how and how much He wants you to give to the ongoing work of the gospel, both globally and locally. If giving feels scary, tell Him about your concerns. Then seek what He has to say back to you through His Word. Philippians 4:19 always inspires me in my giving: "God will meet all your needs according to the riches of his glory in Christ Jesus."

When God called us to love Him first and foremost, and love others second, He didn't make a mistake and forget about us. He knows our needs and promises to meet them when we keep our eyes on Him. Knowing that He will provide our needs frees us up to respond to the needs of those who are physically and spiritually impoverished. It's easier to say yes to Him and no to ourselves when we remember how abundantly stocked His storehouses are.

When you lay down the distraction of self-love, you are freed up to devote yourself to loving God by serving others.

The same is true when we're giving the limited resources of our time and attention away, not only on Sunday morning but all week long. Don't limit your service to the church service but take the church service out into the world by serving. Of course, this takes thinking less of yourself and more of others, whether you are giving your money, time, or attention to meet their needs. As I mentioned earlier, putting yourself last is a type of self-fast. When you lay down the distraction of self-love, you are freed up to devote yourself to loving God by serving others. The spiritual disciplines of tithing and serving will grow the spiritual muscles of your faith as they allow you to share your faith with others.

In the quiet of a prayerful conversation, ask God how He wants you to financially and practically join in the work He's doing both locally and globally. His storehouses are abundantly stocked. Trust that He'll provide all you need as He uses you to provide for the needs of others.

Oh God, my God, Thank You for inviting me to join You in what You're doing in the local church and around the world. Speak to my heart about how to give and how much to give, where to serve and how to serve. It's my heart's desire to respond joyfully, not fearfully. Please give me courage. This isn't a small prayer, God. I'm asking You to make me a more generous giver and servant, because You've given me so much. Amen.

Looking for Ways to Serve and Support?

Reach out to your local church and find out where they need help right now. Do they need Sunday school teachers for the four-year-olds? Greeters at the early service? People to stay around after church and take down tables and chairs on the patio? Small group leaders for the middle school midweek services? Is there a missionary the church knows who is struggling to meet their monthly support? Maybe the cries of those starving in developing nations have reached your ears and your heart? Or maybe there are practical items you can give to the local pregnancy resource center downtown.

Think outside the box and then follow God out of your comfort zone, believing He'll be true to His Word and will provide all you need according to His riches in glory (Phil. 4:19).

DAY 39

Getting Quiet in Order to Hear

The Spiritual Disciplines of Solitude and Meditation

We demolish arguments and every pretension that sets itself up against the knowledge of God, and we take captive every thought to make it obedient to Christ.

2 Corinthians 10:5

The last few days, we've looked at the spiritual practices of prayer and Bible reading, Christian fellowship, and giving and serving, but today's discipline may be the most helpful of all when it comes to growing our devotion: solitude and meditation. Today we are considering what it means to spend time with the One we want to be most devoted to.

No matter what we're fasting from, fasting brings some measure of quiet to our lives. Whether we stop running to every dinner bell or every ding on our phone, fasting settles us down and gives us a chance to sit down. As we take our apps captive, there's a chance we'll take our thoughts captive too. Quietly devoting ourselves to Christ in our thought life is one of the most private yet powerful practices of all the spiritual disciplines.

While devotion amid digital distractions is hard, distracting thoughts are nothing new. Brother Lawrence, a seventeenth-century French monk, wrote:

> I began to live as if there were not one in the world but Him and me. I adored Him as often as I could, keeping my mind in his holy presence and recalling it as often as it wandered. I had no little difficulty in this exercise, but I kept on despite all the difficulties and was not worried or distressed when I was involuntarily distracted. I did this during the day as often as I did it during the formal time specifically set aside for prayer; for at all times, at every hour, at every moment, even in the busiest times of my work, I banished and put away from my mind everything capable of diverting me from the thought of God.[1]

Every time I read this quote, I return to the last few lines: "I banished and put away from my mind everything capable of diverting me from the thought of God." Brother Lawrence desired to be single-minded. He knew nothing of our current culture. He lived among other monks, slept and studied within the confines of four stone walls with only the comfort of a bed and the luxury of a wooden chair beside a simple table. Still, his thoughts worked to divert him, to distract him from his devotion. And so, "at all times, at every hour, at every moment, even in the busiest times" Brother Lawrence devoted himself to focusing his thoughts on God.

Second Corinthians 10:5 admonishes us to "take captive every thought to make it obedient to Christ." Goodness, what a charge!

The New Living Translation tells us that we are to "capture their rebellious thoughts and teach them to obey Christ." The apostle Paul was talking about any thought opposed to Christ at work in our lives and our minds. From negative inner dialogue to sinful fantasies to mildly inappropriate but seemingly harmless humorous thoughts, we're called to take them all captive in strong military language, because Paul knows our minds are spiritual battlefields.

The prince of this world whispers lies in our ears about who we aren't, so we can't hear God's truth telling us who we are.

We are in a spiritual battle. The prince of this world whispers lies in our ears about who we aren't, so we can't hear God's truth telling us who we are. Other times he diverts us with thoughts that are less important so we don't remember what is most important. That's why the Master gave us this muscular command: *Tear down the lies, deny the distractions, and surrender your thoughts to Me.* Our lack of self-control where consumption is concerned is a serious problem, no doubt, but our thought life is out of control too. **God is calling us to set down any thought that is not obedient to Christ.** What would it look like to practice the spiritual discipline of denying other voices in order to hear His? How do we hold our thoughts captive as we hold our apps captive? And is it possible that this spiritual discipline can teach us to live a listening life even after this fast is through?

Opening up the Word is a practical charge; we sort of know what that should look like. Making it to church on Sundays isn't too hard for us to imagine either. Even giving our tithe to the church can be calculated and counted out into the offering plate. But the discipline of holding our thoughts captive so that we might meditate on Christ seems elusive. What are we to think about? What do we actually *do*? And how long do we quietly sit there? If prayer is its own discipline, then what exactly is meditation? Good questions.

I've heard it said that while prayer is talking to God, meditation is simply listening to Him. The discipline of solitude and meditation is about learning to quietly commune with Christ, not just communicate with Him. Thomas Merton wrote, "The deepest level of communication is not communication but communion. It is wordless. It is beyond words, and it is beyond speech, and it is beyond concept."[2]

Christ came that we might know an intimate, devoted relationship with the Father, the Spirit, and Himself. The purpose of solitude isn't that we are solitary; it's to develop a private, intimate love relationship with the One who invites us to come away with Him to a solitary place (see Mark 6:31).

> *The discipline of solitude and meditation is about learning to quietly commune with Christ, not just communicate with Him.*

A. W. Tozer wrote these words to inspire us to pull away from all society, not merely social media, in order to quietly commune with the Lord:

Retire sometimes from the crush of the world, from all human society, including your family. Retire and shut your door, and there alone with God you will grow in grace. You will become calm while the world screams and rattles and blows its terrible whistles around you. When you have had your soul blessed, you can come back down where the poor, tired, noisy world is whistling past its graveyards and talk to them about something worthwhile.[3]

Today, practice silence and solitude. It will be easier to do now than in a few days from now, when the bells are ringing and the whistles are blowing once again. As for now, once you finish this chapter, don't be finished. Remain in your chair. Sit quietly for a few minutes more. **Allow the Spirit of God to speak to your spirit. Commune with Him. Sit in His presence and enjoy the knowledge of His nearness.** Then tonight, before you go to sleep, practice this spiritual discipline again. And in the morning, before you even open your eyes, lie there with Him. Commune with Him in the silence at the start of another day. Devote yourself to this spiritual discipline now, then carry it with you in your life beyond this fast.

There are no one-size-fits-all formulas for any of these disciplines, but they do all take a willingness to rearrange our lives in an effort to grow spiritually stronger. Tozer went on to say,

> I want to rearrange my schedule so that I can retire sometimes from the crushing society for a little time with God, cultivating spiritual things and calming my heart and listening to God speak in the silence. I do not say how frequently. I do not say how long. I just say that something like this has to be done if we are going to break the magnetic attachment of society upon our poor hearts.[4]

Dear Lord, I've taken my apps captive; help me to take my thoughts captive too. I want to submit my whole life, including my thought life, to You. It requires silence and stillness to unpack the noise in my head. Thank You for inviting me to come away with You to a solitary place and sit in silence. Teach me to quiet my mind so that I might know Your mind.

In the quieting, counseling name of Jesus, Amen.

DAY 40

Boundaries and Freedom

It is for freedom that Christ has set us free. Stand firm, then, and do not let yourselves be burdened again by a yoke of slavery.

Galatians 5:1

I find it ironic that our phones are called "cells." All too often, we find ourselves held captive by them and feel like prisoners *locked in our cells*. Today, however, we're celebrating our liberation. Prison doors have sprung open and we're walking in the sunlight now! Here on the last day of your fast, I pray you are experiencing a profound sense of freedom that inspires you to keep standing firm and free in the Son—even after the fast is through.

Your freedom was Christ's reason for coming to earth in the first place. Take one more *Selah* pause and let that incredible reality fill you. He came to grant you freedom from sin's shackles and consequences. He came to set you free to walk at His side into the glorious presence of God the Father. And He left His Spirit behind to guide you in your ongoing free life. Considering the great lengths to which He went to set you free and help you to remain free, what will you choose to do today and tomorrow and the next day?

John 8:36 says, "So if the Son sets you free, you will be free indeed." What plans have you made to protect your freedom? Remember, holy habits don't come naturally or accidentally. Though your freedom was freely given, remaining free may cost you. Are you ready to set some guardrails around your online life so that you don't lose your real life? If you want to keep walking in freedom—with empty hands swinging carefree at your sides, empty hands lifting in worship, empty hands available to hug loved ones and serve others—you've got to have a plan before this day is through.

Go to the Word before the world.

Perhaps you've heard this common expression: "If you fail to plan, you are planning to fail." Before you step back into the digital world, make a plan! **With boundaries firmly in place, you have a better chance of keeping Christ in first place.** Boundaries will help you exchange your online distractions for real-life devotion.

Here are the boundaries I find most helpful:

Go to the Word before the world. Our family has a sign beside the charging station in our room that reads: "The Word before the world." Phones are a portal to the world, but the Bible is a portal to the One who is the Word. Before I open myself up to the opinions of others, I must know what God thinks. Before I look out, I look up. And I am teaching my children to do the same.

Use a printed Bible, not an online version. When I use the Bible app on my phone, I wind up staying on my device for an hour after I've closed that app. Not good. So I have made it a habit to keep a Bible beside my bed or on the kitchen table to help me focus on my priorities at the start of each new day. That said, I do like to use my phone throughout the day as Scriptures come to mind for various reasons. I love how easy it is to do a Google search when I'm reminded of a few words from a familiar passage. However, first thing in the morning and when at church on Sunday mornings, I reach for my old-fashioned, leather-bound friend.

Choose when to be online. Years ago, I asked my husband if he would be willing to join me in putting down our phones from the end of the workday until the kids went to bed. While I still love that idea, I now implement a more effective boundary I learned from Cal Newport in his book *Digital Minimalism*.[1] Instead of choosing an hour or two to put my phone down, I choose the hours when I will pick it up. This doesn't include the rare calls I receive; it's the time I spend on social media. It is a small change that makes a huge difference.

Unfollow people whose posts cause you to feel stress or negativity. If some of your online relationships are unhealthy, now is the time to unfollow those people. There are ways to do this without "unfriending" them. Depending on what social media platform you use, you can block certain people's posts so you don't have to see them during your limited time online. I suggest this for family, friends, and work colleagues who stress you out. There's no need to experience feelings of *dislike* when scrolling through posts from those you "like."

Create a feed that feeds. If and when you decide to return to your favorite social media sites, commit to using that space to bless and encourage others rather than to argue out loud or silently judge. Use your feed to feed others, building others up by your love and good works. You went dark online for a season in order to experience the Light of the World. Now that you've soaked up His presence, you are also a light to the world. Go shine for Him!

Turn off your notifications, hide your apps, or take social media entirely off your phone. These are some of the easiest boundaries you can set. If you did these things at the start of your fasting days, why undo them now? Carefully consider what you want to use social media for, when you want to use it, and how much of your life you're willing to give it. If you have enjoyed your freedom, do whatever it takes to keep walking in it, parenting in it, working in it, and living in it. It was for freedom that Christ set you free, so do what it takes to remain that way. Healthy boundaries aren't intended to bind you up but to free you up!

Take a social media sabbatical every Sunday. This is the best way for me to honor the Sabbath. If God called us to lay down work for one day a week, I imagine that's the day I should lay down my phone as well. #fundaysunday is a popular hashtag, but that doesn't mean you need to share your fun online with everyone. Allow Sundays to be a special time, a private time, and a holy time.

Take a 40-Day Social Media Fast every year. In addition to your weekly sabbatical, choose a time *each year* to step away for forty days. You've done it once; plan to do it again. Forty days is a little more than 10 percent of the year—think of it as tithing your attention and affection.

Keep following the One who set you free. Christ set you free! Stay devoted to Him above all others. Refuse to get distracted. Second Corinthians 3:17 tells us, "Now the Lord is the Spirit, and where the Spirit of the Lord is, there is freedom." Keep the Spirit closer than your phone and seek His wisdom more than any wise words shared on podcasts, master classes, or TED Talks.

If you've experienced any measure of joy as you've devoted yourself to God's presence, don't casually hop back online tomorrow as though it won't impact your intimate relationship with Him. It will. Be careful and be prayerful. While this is the end of your fast, it shouldn't be the end of your freedom. Don't allow yourself to get tangled up in all those charging cords again, or you may trip over them and fall right back into that old cell.

Healthy boundaries aren't intended to bind you up but to free you up!

As you intentionally set your boundaries, keep the spiritual disciplines we've covered a priority in your life. You don't need to fast 365 days a year, but those holy habits must be part of your year-round routine if you want to continue standing firm. Even when your fast is through, you must remember to keep ingesting God's Word and practicing His presence.

Fasting isn't a once-and-done spiritual practice. If you find yourself distracted, forgetting to consume the eternal things, fast again from things that are temporarily distracting you in order to remember. **The point of fasting is always feasting. When you stop consuming the temporary things of this world, you're free to feast on the eternal presence of the One who made the world.** Our goal these forty days was not to merely eliminate online distractions but to grow in our freedom and devotion to the Lord as we enjoy Him and all His blessings [IRL]. This fast might be over but your freedom should never end.

Dear Lord, I am so glad I had this undistracted time with You. I used to get anxious if my phone would lose its charge, but now that I've been charged by the right power source, I'm experiencing peace and freedom! Help me to set boundaries around this free and peaceful life You've given me, so that I don't get tangled up and tripped up again.

In the bondage-breaking name of Jesus, Amen.

DAY 41

A Lifetime of Devotion

My counsel for you is simple and straightforward: Just go ahead with what you've been given. You received Christ Jesus, the Master; now *live* him. You're deeply rooted in him. You're well constructed upon him. You know your way around the faith. Now do what you've been taught. School's out; quit studying the subject and start *living* it!

Colossians 2:6–7 MSG

I added a bonus chapter because the goal of this fast isn't to take a short "break" or even a permanent "breakup" from social media. The goal of fasting—always—is more of Jesus. More of Jesus crowding out everyone and everything else that's been getting in our way, distracting us, and giving us a false sense of fullness. **If your life is full of Him now, there isn't as much room for the things you once turned to habitually.** He's your habit, your new habit, your holy habit! Life should be different today than it was forty-one days ago. If it is, then I suggest you don't slide right back to where you were. Carefully consider how you want your life, both online and offline, to look.

Now that Christ is securely seated at the center of your life, keep Him there. Don't go back to your old life, living most of every day online. Keep your eyes on Him. In *The Art of Racing in the Rain*, Garth Stein warns us, "Your car goes where your eyes go."[1] That's our warning today: our lives go where our eyes go. We spent the first days of this fast lifting our eyes to God and found Him alive and well in nature and in our closest relationships. We discovered Him at work and at play, and even at the grocery store. Lifting our eyes from our screens allowed us to feel seen and to see. Averting our eyes from online distractions was the first step to rediscovering a life of devotion, but in order to sustain that life, we must keep our eyes lifted.

> Now that Christ is securely seated at the center of your life, keep Him there.

Simply limiting your distractions for forty days won't keep you devoted to God for the rest of your days—though it may help. Instead, start with a devoted life, with your eyes on Him 365 days of the year, and He will help you deal with any distractions as they come. When your eyes are on Christ first and foremost, everything else finds its proper place. But when something else takes first place, it's nearly impossible to find a place for Him. That's what we're talking about today. Not forty days of devotion but a lifetime of devotion, with Christ at the center, crowding out the distractions. He never asked for forty days but rather an eternity as King of your heart. Have you given Him your heart?

Decide to do that now, if you haven't already. School's out; this is your graduation day! This is the start of life beyond your fast. The boundaries we talked about yesterday will help, but Christ at the center of your life helps more. When temptation comes, He's there to defend His rightful place. You are His dwelling place. Stay committed to that intimate relationship above any other. Get social with Him before you turn to social media each morning.

The passage below always comes to mind as I fast from anything that has taken higher rank in my life than it should. Let me encourage you to grab a pen and circle any words that reference Christ's preeminent position in our hearts and lives.

> The Son is the image of the invisible God, the *firstborn* over all creation. For in him all things were created: things in heaven and on earth, visible and invisible, whether thrones or powers or rulers or authorities; all things have been created through him and for him. He is *before* all things, and in him all things hold together. And he is the *head* of the body, the church; he is the *beginning* and the *firstborn* from among the dead, so that in everything he might have the supremacy. (1 Col. 1:15–18, emphasis added)

Before anything else was created, Christ existed, and through Him everything else came into existence. He was first and the firstborn. The head of the body of believers, the head of the church. The very tip-top. The beginning. Therefore, before we turn to anyone or anything else each day, we must turn to Him. Christ must continue to hold first place in our days. Yesterday, I shared that one of my own personal boundaries is to turn to the Word before I turn to the world each morning. The Word before the world. It is the most practical way I keep Christ in first place in my life, literally before all else.

There is much to do and many people to respond to, but I believe Jesus when He said, "But seek first [God's] kingdom and his righteousness, and all these things will be given to you as well" (Matt. 6:33).

The distractions of this world seem so important to us all the time, don't they? Emails must be answered, sporting events must be attended, kids need to get to school, we need to get to work, shopping trips must be made, dinners have to be cooked, dishes need to get done, and laundry is always on repeat. The new season of your favorite show and the latest episodes of your favorite podcasts will both drop into your virtual lap today too. And yet Christ must continue to have supremacy. **First Christ and then everything else. That's the order of our days.** Press into Him and pursue Him every morning and throughout the day.

> Pursue the things over which Christ presides. Don't shuffle along, eyes to the ground, absorbed with the things right in front of you. Look up, and be alert to what is going on around Christ—that's where the action is. See things from *his* perspective. (Col. 3:1–2 MSG)

This passage appeared at the beginning of the book, on the dedication page. I'm ending with it too, because lifting our eyes, lifting our heads, and lifting our hands to Him in worship and to others in service is what this real life is all about. This is where the action is! Don't stumble along; look up. When you live with your eyes up, you'll be less likely to trip up! Forty days of devotion was never the goal. We're after a lifetime of devotion.

Forty days of devotion was never the goal. We're after a lifetime of devotion.

It has been my joy to journey with you during these quiet days offline. While I have led you into the Word, Christ is the One who is the Word, and He's leading us now. Follow Him. Before you turn your gaze back to everyone else you're following, stay committed to following Him!

God, I'm so glad I had this time with You. I'm beginning to understand that it doesn't have to end now. Time with You for forty days was just the beginning. That was the point of these fasting days, wasn't it? You don't want just forty days at the center of my life; You want all my days centered around You. That's the life I'm devoted to now. Help me to stay the course as distractions come, Lord. For I am Yours and You are mine.

If I forget, I'll fast again in order to remember.

In Jesus's name, Amen.

Acknowledgments

I humbly acknowledge that I could not have written one word worth reading without the help of the Holy Spirit. Nor could I have finished the task without the sacrificial support of my loving family, the faithful prayers of my dear friends, and the continued hard work of the publishing team God has so generously provided.

I am overwhelmed with gratitude.

To my husband, Matt: thank you for embracing me so tenderly and, in so doing, embracing this calling on my life as well. It hasn't been easy. I recognize that when I pull away to serve others, I sometimes pull away from you. You are dear to help me dance this awkward dance of serving at home and beyond our home. Thank you for building me a she-shed writing studio and taking the boys camping, switching out laundry, and doing the dishes. Any fruit that comes from my labor is because we colabored.

To my agent, Bill Jensen: God must really love me to give me you. You're the best literary agent in the whole wide world! To my editor, Liz Heaney: I keep growing as a writer as you challenge me. To the incredible team at Baker Publishing: I am continually blessed by your ongoing support, enthusiasm, and affirmation. Here's to serving together again!

Finally, to those who read this book: your desire to want the World Wide Web less and the One who made the world more was my driving motivator. I want to want God most as well. It is a privilege to seek Him and find Him with you.

Notes

Before You Fast

1. C. S. Lewis, *Mere Christianity* (New York: Macmillan, 1952), 53.
2. John Piper, "Ask Pastor John: When Should I Get Rid of My Smartphone?" *Desiring God*, August 25, 2015, https://www.desiringgod.org/interviews/when-should-i-get-rid-of-my-smartphone.
3. "Average Time Spent on Social Media," Broadband Search, accessed June 18, 2020, https://www.broadbandsearch.net/blog/average-daily-time-on-social-media.
4. As quoted in Nemanja Jovancic, "55 Social Media Quotes about Twitter, LinkedIn, and Facebook Marketing," *Lead Quizzes*, August 31, 2018, https://www.leadquizzes.com/blog/55-social-media-quotes-on-twitter-linkedin-and-facebook-marketing/.

Day 1 Is Social Media Bad?

1. C. S. Lewis, *Christian Reflections* (Grand Rapids: Eerdmans, 1967), 33.
2. A. W. Tozer, "Counsel for Faith's Journey," *Gems from Tozer: Selections from the Writings of A. W. Tozer* (Chicago: Moody, 2017).

Day 3 Escapism

1. "2853. kollaó," Bible Hub, accessed June 19, 2020, https://biblehub.com/strongs/greek/2853.htm.
2. Andy Crouch, *The Tech-Wise Family* (Grand Rapids: Baker Books, 2017), 26–27.
3. Arlene Pellicane, *Calm, Cool, and Connected: 5 Digital Habits for a More Balanced Life* (Chicago: Moody, 2017), 58.

Day 4 Getting Social [IRL]

1. "Johann Wolfgang von Goethe Quotable Quotes," Goodreads, accessed June 19, 2020, https://www.goodreads.com/quotes/2326-things-which-matter-most.

Day 7 Eyes on the Skies

1. "Ann Voskamp's Blog, Page 21: July 6, 2019," Goodreads, accessed June 19, 2020, https://www.goodreads.com/author/show/1890390.Ann_Voskamp/blog?page=21._.

Day 9 Spring Cleaning

1. "Idioms and Phrases: Cleanliness Is Next to Godliness," Dictionary.com, accessed June 19, 2020, https://www.dictionary.com/browse/cleanliness-is-next-to-godliness.

Day 11 Get Your Phone off His Throne

1. Ruth Chou Simons and Troy Simons, *Foundations* (Eugene, OR: Harvest House, 2019), 28.

Day 12 Tech-Neck

1. David DeWitt, "How Does Text Neck Cause Pain?" Spine-health, October 26, 2018, https://www.spine-health.com/conditions/neck-pain/how-does-text-neck-cause-pain.

Day 13 Golden Nuggets

1. Alisha Illian, *Chasing Perfect* (Eugene, OR: Harvest House, 2020), 15.

Day 14 Stop Scrolling, Start Strolling

1. "In the Garden," Charles A. Miles (1913), public domain.

Day 15 Fill My Cup, Lord

1. "Fill My Cup, Lord," Richard Blanchard (1959), copyright renewed 1988 by Word Music, LLC. All rights reserved.

Day 17 Chosen

1. Tony Reinke, "Know When to Walk Away: A Twelve-Step Digital Detox," *Desiring God*, May 30, 2016, https://www.desiringgod.org/articles/know-when-to-walk-away.

Day 22 Are You Ready to Be God-Ready?

1. Kaushik Patowary, "Shrek, the Sheep Who Escaped Shearing for 6 Years," *Amusing Planet*, July 23, 2014, https://www.amusingplanet.com/2014/07/shrek-sheep-who-escaped-shearing-for-6.html.

Day 23 Keeping Your First Love First

1. Matt Lindner, "Does Using Social Media Make You More Likely to Cheat?" *Chicago Tribune*, November 11, 2016, https://www.chicagotribune.com/lifestyles/sc-social-media-cheating-family-1115-20161111-story.html.

2. Joyce Marter as quoted in Linder, "Does Using Social Media."

Day 25 Savor the Savior

1. John Piper, *A Hunger for God: Desiring God through Fasting and Prayer* (Wheaton: Crossway, 1997), 23.

2. Evangelist Reinhard Bonnke—Official Page, Facebook post, January 8, 2011, https://www.facebook.com/evangelistreinhardbonnke/posts/the-less-holy-spirit-we-have-the-more-cake-and-coffee-we-need-to-keep-the-church/155190414531578/.

Day 29 Extra! Extra! Read All about It!

1. "National Human & Sex Trafficking Statistics," Geoffrey G. Nathan Law Offices, accessed June 19, 2020, https://www.geoffreygnathanlaw.com/topics/national-human-trafficking-statistics/.

Day 30 Little Foxes

1. Ole Hallesby, *Prayer*, updated ed. (Minneapolis: Augsburg Fortress, 1994), 114.

Day 33 Holy Habits

1. Crouch, *Tech-Wise Family*, 37.

Day 35 Dress Rehearsal

1. Leonard Ravenhill, *Why Revival Tarries* (Bloomington, MN: Bethany, 2007), 19.
2. Stormie Omartian, *The Power of a Praying Wife* (Eugene, OR: Harvest House, 1997).
3. "Andrew Bonar Quotes," *Christian Quotes*, accessed June 19, 2020, https://www.christianquotes.info/quotes-by-author/andrew-bonar-quotes/.

Day 36 Take Me to Church

1. Lisa Whittle "JOE S3E8: Interview with Beth Moore," January 28, 2020, https://lisawhittle.com/joe-s3e8.
2. "1577. ekklésia," Bible Hub, accessed June 19, 2020, https://biblehub.com/greek/1577.htm.

Day 37 Going Dark

1. Lisa Whittle, Instagram post, October 24, 2019, https://www.instagram.com/p/B3_9c37BjnY/.
2. "Trust and Obey," John Henry Sammis (1887), public domain.

Day 39 Getting Quiet in Order to Hear

1. As quoted in Shane Claiborne, Jonathan Wilson-Hartgrove, and Enuma Okoro, *Common Prayer: A Liturgy for Ordinary Radicals* (Grand Rapids: Zondervan, 2010), 252–53.
2. Thomas Merton, *The Hidden Ground of Love: Letters*, ed. William H. Shannon (New York: Farrar, Straus & Giroux, 1985), x.
3. A. W. Tozer, *No Greater Love* (Bloomington, MN: Bethany House, 2020), 102.
4. Tozer, *No Greater Love*, 102–3.

Day 40 Boundaries and Freedom

1. Cal Newport, *Digital Minimalism* (New York: Portfolio, 2019).

Day 41 A Lifetime of Devotion

1. Garth Stein, *The Art of Racing in the Rain* (New York: HarperCollins, 2011), 83.

Wendy Speake is the author of *The 40-Day Sugar Fast* and *The 40-Day Fast Journal*, and is coauthor of *Triggers: Exchanging Parents' Angry Reactions for Gentle Biblical Responses*. Wendy hosts her annual online 40-Day Sugar Fast every January and her 40-Day Social Media Fast every Lent. She lives in Escondido, California. Learn more at www.wendyspeake.com.

Ready to Go — DEEPER?

Join the annual online 40-DAY SUGAR FAST.

Every January, author Wendy Speake leads a group of
Jesus-hungry men and women through forty days of fasting
from sugar in order to feast together on the satisfying
sweetness of our Savior! Join the private Facebook group
for a powerful and transformative experience.

Visit **40daysugarfast.com**
to SIGN UP for our next community-wide fast.

Connect with
BakerBooks
Relevant. Intelligent. Engaging.

Sign up for announcements about
new and upcoming titles at

BakerBooks.com/SignUp

@ReadBakerBooks